Leadership from the Inside Out – Are You the Leader YOU Would Follow?

Kris Barney

ISBN:
ISBN-13 978-0-9881882-7-3:

Acknowledgements

First and foremost, I want to acknowledge my husband of 35 years, Bill Barney. His dedication, wisdom, insight, patience, love and intuition have been an incredible support for me both through the process of writing this book as well as the grueling years of living and learning what this book is all about. I am who I am in great part by the influence and love of this incredible man.

To my phenomenal parents, Lee and Nikki Brady, for their values, character and skills that they instilled in me as they taught me the value of work, the value of service and the value of striving to be the best I could be. For believing in me and loving me for whom I am and what I have become.

To my amazing children and grandchildren-for all that you have taught me. You make me want to be a better Mother and Grandmother. What an honor and privilege it is to love you and learn from you. We have been through many challenges together and for this I am grateful. We have also been through more joy and happiness than I could have ever imagined together and for this I will always have wonderful fond memories. We have a closeness that is very rare and I treasure that. We love unconditionally and are always supportive and true to each other. I love you all with all my heart!

To Dan Clark, who has been an Icon and Hero for me in this industry for years, that took his precious time and energy to read this manuscript, capture my vision and eloquently and powerfully write the foreword for this book. My appreciation for him and the honor and respect I have for him are hard to put into words. Thank you for believing in me, supporting me and being The Art of Significance in my life.

To Ty Bennett, who is a phenomenal mentor, coach, supporter and dear trusted friend. The Title for this book: Leadership from the Inside Out came to be from you and your influence with me. I am where I am today as a speaker and trainer through your belief in me and your direction. I love your example and your influence. You have been an incredible piece to this puzzle. Partnership has truly been the new Leadership!

To my Editor, Tiffany Fletcher. My gratitude and love runs deep. Thank you for your diligence and time spent to edit this book, to bring it together in harmony and balance and making it all that it is. This book will bless many lives and I have you to thank for being such an integral part in creating it to come to fruition.

To my Graphic Design, web design and book cover, Kiersten Nebeker. You brought this together with the branding, the design, and final package. I have had you do a lot for me and value your talents so highly. You have pulled this all together and made us look really great! You are dedicated and true and you have been amazing to work with and become a trusted friend. I always look better when you have had anything to do with it!

To my formatter, Erin McBride. You have been with us

for all three books now. You are great at pulling it all together and putting the bow on top. I am not sure if we have ever had a conversation during normal business hours, as we are always talking at close to midnight, finalizing every piece and putting it all together. Thank you for your skill and ability to do the finishing touches! You are Fantastic!

To Redd Printing-Eric Redd you have always done exceptional work for us and yes, we are now having you print our third book! Thank you for being willing and able to jump through hoops and time restraints to make it all come together and be pulled off fabulously! We know that we can trust you and your business with our printing and fulfillment of orders. You have been incredible to work with.

To many Dear Trusted Friends, fellow Speakers and Authors, my Mastermind Crew and phenomenal people that have been willing to pre-read this book, write glowing endorsements and give me solid and valuable advice, to Cheryl Knowlton, Jason Hall, Brad Barton, Dr. Paul Jenkins and Kordell Norton, I am forever in your debt! Thank you for being all that you are. Thank you for assisting me to step up and forge forward continually. Thank you for your support, encouragement and your love. I truly am blessed.

And finally...I wish to acknowledge my Heavenly Father. It is through him that I know this book was supposed to be. It is through him that All Things are Possible and that I have been able to put this book together. I know I have been given the challenges in my life to learn and to grow and it is through my Heavenly Father that I know my mission and passion are to share it with you. I am all that I am through him.

Advance Praise for *Leadership from the Inside Out – Are You the Leader YOU Would Follow?*

"Leadership has always been an Inside Out process. As you change as a leader, your influence grows and your impact increases. Every Leader would do well to read this book and do the inner work that will add to your outward effectiveness and influence. Embrace the 7 Traits that Kris has developed and watch as you transform your confidence, relationships, and your success."

~Ty Bennett, Author of "Partnership is the New Leadership"

"The principles and traits Kris shares in her book are dynamic, true, and can be life-changing for those who apply them. If leaders follow these simple truths, not only will they understand how to make the necessary changes to have a successful and productive business, but they will have a greater understanding and a deeper connection to those they lead. They will truly become the leader that others will want to follow.

~Tiffany Fletcher, Speaker and Author of "Mother Had a Secret" and "Turn Your Light On"

"In this must have book, Kris Barney has put together powerful stories and lessons about how to overcome real challenges. If you'll live these principles, you'll find that you'll become, THE LEADER THAT YOU WOULD FOLLOW.

~Jason Hall, Speaker, Author and Expert in "Conquering your Threshold"

"Get ready to become your best self! Through Kris' extraordinary ability to share personal and vulnerable life lessons, she teaches us 7 Timeless Traits that if implemented, will transform lives and create exceptional Leaders."

~Cheryl Knowlton, CSP, DREI

"A heartfelt and personal journey into the mind of a true leader. Kris, You Nailed It!"

~Brad Barton, CSP Author of "Beyond Illusions"

"Kris your new book poses a question for each of us to reflect on and truthfully answer for ourselves! It outlines realistic perspectives and processes for individuals and corporate leaders alike! Businesses and corporations who implement your 7 Traits will improve their leadership skills and create a trusting environment for each of their team members."

~Kiersten Nebeker CEO of K Marketing Creative; Corporate Branding and Organizational Development

"Kris Barney brings an authentic, real and fresh approach to a topic that too often is stale and routine. She gives us a leadership recipe that is both practical and psychologically sound. Get ready to power-up your leadership from the inside out!"

~Dr. Paul Jenkins, Positivity Psychologist

"Educational, mixed with common sense, and entertaining stories. Here is a book for dealing with the internal challenges that individual Leaders face. This is a highlighter read for sure!"

~Kordell N Norton, CSP President, Synergy Solutions, LLC & "America's Charisma Consultant"

TABLE OF CONTENTS

Acknowledgements i
Advance Praise v
Dedication xi
Foreword by Dan Clark xiii
Introduction xviii
TRAIT ONE: SHOW Sincere Service 1
Chapter 1: Simple Service vs Sincere Service 3
Chapter 2: What She Taught Me at Nine, Saved Me at Twenty-Nine 17
Chapter 3: What He Learned at Nine Changed Us Forever 25
TRAIT TWO: GROW in Genuine Gratitude 39
Chapter 4: Generic Gratitude vs Genuine Gratitude 41
Chapter 5: Her Death Opened My Eyes 53
Chapter 6: Empathy and Gratitude in the Workplace 59
TRAIT THREE: CREATE Courageous Confidence 67
Chapter 7: Cowardly Confidence vs. Courageous Confidence 69
Chapter 8: Who Are You Listening to Anyway—Believe in You 75
Chapter 9: Happiness is a Choice 83
TRAIT FOUR: EXCEL in Exceptional Excellence 91
Chapter 10: Enough Excellence vs. Extraordinary Excellence 93
Chapter 11: Exceptional Excellence in the Workplace 101
Chapter 12: Oh That Brother of Mine 107
TRAIT FIVE: LIVE in Lasting Love 113
Chapter 13: Limited Love vs Lasting Love 115
Chapter 14: Holy Crap! Our Son is Gay! 123

Chapter 15 What One Sows, One Reaps 131
TRAIT SIX: CONNECT in Complete Communication 139
Chapter 16: Confusing Communication vs Complete Communication 141
Chapter 17: The Power in Good Communication 155
Chapter 18: Are You Really Listening? 161
TRAIT SEVEN: IMPLEMENT Impeccable Integrity 167
Chapter 19: Inconsistent Integrity or Impeccable Integrity 169
Chapter 20: What Are Ethics Anyway 181
Chapter 21: A Year to Remember 189
CONCLUSION 199
Quotes 203
Testimonials 213
About the Author 215

Dedication

I dedicate this book to all those who desire to be a more influential leader, no matter their position. Be a better manager, team player, spouse, parent, friend, and individual. Be the Leader YOU Would Follow! I dedicate this to you, my reader and to your ability to be the very best you can be.

Foreword

In my 35+ years as a professional speaker I know that the way to create an extraordinary meeting is to make sure the reason is relevant, the message is provocative and the speaker has lived the message, so your people leave with tools and benefits that will impact both their professional and personal relationships long after the meeting adjourns.

This 'gold standard' also applies to writing an extraordinary book – especially in vetting the message against the messenger, asking: 'Does the author live the message?'

In my Public Speaking Boot Camps I teach my students that everybody in every audience craves the answers to three fundamental questions: (1) Why should I listen to you? Have you done it? Are you currently doing it? This is the 'Credibility' piece. (2) Can I do it too? With my weaknesses and limitations and strengths? This is the 'Possibility' piece. (3) How do I do it? What do I do next? What is the system? This is the 'Usability' piece.

In this magnificent book, not only will you get the answers to all three of these questions, but you will get the amalgamated knowledge, wisdom and life lessons learned from an amazing human being (who happens to be an incredible woman – not a female leader, but an extraordinary leader who happens to be a woman), wife, mother, sister, teacher, mentor, influencer, colleague and trusted friend who epitomizes Leadership From The Inside Out.

Clearly Kris understands the Law of Attraction in its most provocative application, knowing 'we don't attract who we want – we attract who we are – people do what they see, not what we say' - we attract what we believe we deserve' - in personal and professional relationships, in meaningful work, and in health and wellness. Although profound in her insights, the subliminal message in every chapter is the subtle reminder that: 'People don't care how much you know until they know how much you care.'

I've known Kris for many years and have watched her exemplify 'Inside Out Leadership' – living life as the same person off stage as she is on stage – always beautiful inside and out. By her actions Kris proves leadership is an action verb, not a noun, with her delightful sense of humor pointing out: 'Standing in the front of a room and calling yourself a leader, no more makes you a leader than standing in the middle of a garage makes you a truck.' Leadership implies action! Just as trust, respect and admiration are earned through consistent, predictable, ethical, moral, trustworthy conduct, becoming a 'Leader People Want To Follow' is earned through consistently living the poetic words of Edgar A. Guest:

I'd rather see a sermon than hear one any day
I'd rather one should walk with me than merely tell the way
The eye is a better pupil, more willing than the ear
Fine counsel is confusing, but example's always clear
And the best of all the preachers are those who live their creeds,

For to see good put in action is what everybody needs.

The way you become a leader everyone loves, trusts, respects, admires and follows, is to first become the person whom YOU love, trust, respect, admire and would follow!

I never realized the depth of this reality until the first time I went 'down range' to Iraq and Afghanistan, when a Navy Seal taught me that: 'An armored up warrior never has to get ready – he stays ready!' In other words, you don't just click on character and then click it off. You don't just click on loyalty, excellence, positive attitude, duty, enthusiasm, respect, service before self, honor, integrity and personal courage. These core values and governing principles are part of your DNA that you think and breathe and live by every day. Life is not a dress rehearsal – you never really practice, you only play! In sports, you don't win championships with the best players - you win with the right people. Leadership from the outside in must be exactly the same as leadership from the inside out, or it's not leadership at all.

As you read and re-read this carefully crafted book you will realize that the culture of any organization is shaped by a combination of the worst attitude, worst behavior and weakest belief the leader is willing to tolerate - AND by the most positive attitude, positive behavior and strongest belief the leader is willing to live by! In between the bottom line of tolerance and the top line of example lies the fact that it is the attitude and behavior of the leader that creates the standard of performance expectation for everybody in the group or team – as a parent at home, a teacher at school, a manager/boss at work, and a friend at play.

For this reason, this is a 'must read' for corporate executives, seasoned administrators, emerging leaders, educators, parents, coaches and everyone who wants to be a better leader - with and without a title. When we live by the Seven Traits of Service, Gratitude, Confidence, Excellence, Love, Communication and Integrity, leadership becomes automatic as a philosophical way of living life to the max, proving true that inspired people don't have to be motivated!

If you want to become the 'Leader People Want To Follow,' my recommendation is that you first read this masterfully written book from cover to cover and ponder the practical application of each of the Seven Traits, illuminated by their accompanying three explanatory chapters. Then, with the mindset that you don't learn to know – you learn to do, you obligate yourself to live the Seven Traits beginning on a Monday with Trait #1. Followed on Tuesday by only focusing on living Trait #2. On Wednesday you live Trait #3, and so on until the week is over and you have experienced the profound effect of knowing it is not enough to just practice what you preach. You must preach only what you practice! Then repeat.

Thank God that Kris took the time to show her genuine love for each of us by compiling her years of education and personal experience into this powerful book that reminds us that the only way we can attract high quality, extraordinary human beings into our lives and recruit them to work in our organizations, is if we are high quality, extraordinary human beings! By the time you click off your reading light you will know that the only real and authentic, lasting way that any of us can influence people to become the best version of them self is through Leadership from the Inside Out!

Dan Clark
Hall of Fame Speaker
New York Times Best Selling Author of
'The Art of Significance – Achieving the Level Beyond Success'

Introduction

Leadership from the Inside Out - Are You the Leader YOU Would Follow?

When you hear the words "Leadership from the Inside Out," what comes to your mind? When I have asked this before, people have responded with very differing views and meanings. In this book, I want to share with you what "Leadership from the Inside Out" means to me, how I see it differently than most, and why I feel that implementing the 7 Traits found in this book will CHANGE your life—and your world.

There is so much included when we use the term Leadership, and it could even mean different things for different people. The traditional dictionary definition goes something like this:

"Leadership is the position or function of a leader; a person who guides or directs a group. It is in management, administration, directorship, control, governorship, stewardship, authoritativeness, influence, command, effectiveness, sway and clout."

Leadership encompasses all of these definitions. But it is my personal opinion that they have neglected to list the more powerful and more personal parts of being an Exceptional Leader. I believe that a true leader develops qualities and attributes that they hold as a standard, and then exemplify those qualities such as:

- honor
- integrity
- inspiration
- gratitude
- confidence
- influence
- courage
- motivation
- service minded
- strong character
- filled with lasting love
- exceptional excellence
- strong beliefs and values
- trustworthiness and dependability

As you can see, while the dictionary focuses on outward functions of a leader, I have a different perspective on this topic. From my own experiences, I know—and absolutely believe—Exceptional Leadership starts from the inside and moves outward.

In the world of business and society, a manager manages, a governor governs, an administrator administrates, and a director directs. In the same fashion, an Exceptional Leader leads—and they lead through loving example. Everything about this person is honorable and we all want to be more like them, because they truly care about others. To be that Exceptional Leader, we must show it through our efforts to improve ourselves.

"Real Influence Begins with you and is Developed from the Inside Out!" ~Kris Barney

Leadership is not a destination but an ongoing quest. A person will never just arrive at a point and say, "I am done." In fact, it is quite the opposite. Think about a leader who you admire. Have they ever stopped working to improve themselves? NO! Leaders strive to grow and master skills that provide opportunities for improvement and success. This ongoing effort is a change in mindset, a shift in belief, and a willingness to make it a way of life. Exceptional Leaders focus on continuous improvement and personal development. Learning new behaviors and skills builds quality leadership, and they share it everywhere they go.

As our Leadership is developed, our influence expands and we become influential to others. To have a profound impact, you must be willing to continually evaluate and find areas for growth and development.

- As you grow and move forward, your influence expands.
- As your influence expands, you become an impactful leader.
- As your leadership improves, your organization becomes stronger and more profitable, your relationships improve, your health improves, and you truly love your own life.
- Your success is incredible in all areas of your life, and things more naturally tend to go your way.

Change from the Inside Out is how this is created! When we are willing to change, and strive for higher goals and a more defined way of life, we naturally become a Leader.

Think about it. . . **Are you the leader that YOU would follow?**

When we become the leader that we would follow, that is when influence and effectiveness meet. It takes honoring ourselves, and believing in, and being a steward of—our own self.

Let me be clear—you can be a more powerful and influential leader by believing in yourself, staying in impeccable integrity, and holding yourself to higher standards. Taking responsibility for yourself truly does make a profound difference.

When we look back through history, and we strive to find those who have been of highest influence, we see that many of our greatest leaders had all of these qualities and values—and lived them from the Inside Out.

Think of Mahatma Gandhi, Mother Teresa, Martin Luther King, Albert Einstein, Abraham Lincoln, Walt Disney, St Joan of Arc, George Washington, Zig Ziglar, Tony Robbins, and Jim Rohn. This is, of course, just a tip of the iceberg of the influential people who have left a lasting legacy. They have truly had a profound impact on our society and the world.

I am sure that you have your own list of outstanding leaders and treasure what they mean to you. Think about what a difference just these few people have done to make your world different and better. Think of the incredible impact these Exceptional Leaders have had, and the profound difference they have made in the lives of literally thousands and thousands of people. Can you imagine what would happen in our world if even 10% of the population exemplified these phenomenal traits and modeled their lives after Exceptional Leaders?

On the flip side, there are some extremely successful people who really did have it all—EXCEPT for living the inner qualities that establish true leaders. These were popular personalities, who perhaps said it, but did not live it. It is very likely that they were a wreck on the inside and it showed up on the outside. Think of Tiger Woods, O.J. Simpson, or Lance Armstrong. Even huge business icons like Enron's collapse, or even Pan Am Airlines. I am sure that this list could go on forever.

It is not my intention to bring attention to the negatives that came of these, but it proves that when we build our leadership on a solid basis of character, values, and principles—or from the **INSIDE OUT**—we have sustained success and happiness. We are more effective and more productive in all areas of our life! We become the kind of leaders that others naturally follow. **WE BECOME THE LEADER WE WOULD FOLLOW!**

Exceptional Leadership does not come in a pill you can take. Your beliefs, values, and principles cannot be borrowed or forced from someone else. You must develop them deep inside of your being as part of the core of who you are. Other people can influence you to strive to be better—to be all that you can be—and they can motivate you to want those killer results. But it truly does come down to YOU doing the work, implementing what you have learned, and taking your life to the next level. YOU MUST OWN IT! You get to continually up-level and improve yourself to greatness. Owning it becomes second nature once you have implemented the work, and have created the belief behind it.

Let me ask you this: "As a leader, company, family, or individual, do we typically change when things are going well?"

The answer is no. No, we do not. Change needs a catalyst.

- *We change when we are at the end of our rope.*
- *We change when the going gets tough.*
- *We change when there is too much pain to continue doing things the way we have always done them.*

Why not make the decision to change your own life *before* the pain is too heavy, or *before* you feel it is broken? Why not strive for excellence because that is what motivates you? Do you realize that as you change, people respond better to you? They begin to see more of your qualities, because that is what you are showing them. I realize that this is pretty heavy stuff, but it is the ugly truth. We have to be willing to really look at it for what it is.

The truth is—we all respond better to influence than authority. *Authority is never the winner* when compared to Influence. A person who is compelled to action by one in authority will only do the bare minimum; whereas a person who is inspired to take action by an influential leader, will do their personal best. This is because the leader's influence has become an integral part of those they lead.

We all hate to be forced to do something we don't really want to do. It leaves us feeling powerless, and we generally avoid situations and people who make us feel this way. We despise those that try to force us to do things—even if what we're being forced to do is essentially good for us. We do not like being forced period.

But we thrive in an environment that allows us to follow influence. We will go to extreme lengths to do anything asked of us, if the person asking is influential and a good leader. The best leaders we will ever have are those who live life by example—those who hold it in their heart, who stand for what they believe, and live up to their values—those who live from the Inside Out!

To become an Exceptional Leader, I believe there are 7 Traits, that if learned and applied, will CHANGE YOU. They will change your Life—and your World. I have found people who have not only become strengthened and empowered, but have complete transformations, and exceptional success in their life, and in business, when they apply these 7 Traits. This book is a compilation of those 7 Traits—the very same traits that I personally incorporated into my own life when the going got really tough in my world. And I continue to use these traits daily to propel my life forward.

I share these traits with you in the form of a frank conversation. In this book, I share in-depth definitions of each trait, and how to incorporate these traits easily into your life. You will read several personal stories to show some of the ways I learned these traits, and how they have become a huge part of who I am. This was not something I dreamt up overnight. In fact, it came through many years of extremely difficult circumstances in my life. It came from difficult trials and struggles, all while being a multiple business owner, a mother, a wife, and a woman still keeping it together.

I have been a real estate investor, a businesswoman and entrepreneur for 35 years. I am also a business investor, and I am currently an owner of three successful Corporations. I have trained hundreds of clients one-on-

one, and have spoken to tens of thousands from stage. I have furthered my education in not only college, but the school of hard knocks. These 7 Traits have come from years of personal development, and thousands of hours in trainings and conferences. They have been developed through mentoring and training hundreds, if not thousands, of people. These 7 Traits are something I know to be true and I am excited to share them with you.

Here are the 7 Traits you will be learning. The first word of each trait is an acronym, used to describe the trait. You will learn more about these acronyms as you read about them in the chapters:

- SHOW Sincere Service
- GROW in Genuine Gratitude
- CREATE Courageous Confidence
- EXCEL in Exceptional Excellence
- LIVE in Lasting Love
- CONNECT with Complete Communication
- IMPLEMENT Impeccable Integrity

There is not a particular order with the above list, but what I can tell you is that as you develop these traits from within yourself and implement them in your life, the other traits show up on the outside. You will find that creating excellence on the inside, also creates exceptional success on the outside! You become a person of *influence and inspiration* rather than a person of *authority*. Isn't that what we really want anyway?

I'd like you to go back in time with me to June, 2012. My oldest son and I were in the doctor's office. They had taken us back to a room and sat us down. They said the doctor would be in shortly.

The brain surgeon walked in shortly after. He was a young, confident doctor, and had become very familiar with us over the past several months. He walked over to the other side of the room, faced us, and then leaned back against the counter before crossing his legs at the ankles. That's when I noticed the tear in his eye. He looked us in the eyes, and with deep sadness and regret said, "The brain tumor has grown back." **For the THIRD time in just five months!**

This cannot be happening! How much can one child handle? How much could I handle? How could this be? All I could think was, "Holy Crap! How are we EVER going to be able to handle this?"

By this time, my son had turned 26 years old, but this was a far cry from our first onset of trouble. Our family had been through some really hard times before, and it had shaped us for what lied ahead.

For many years in my life, I wondered why these tough challenges just kept piling up for us. But it wasn't until after this one that I finally put some common denominators together to understand what an impact these difficulties had on my life. How was I able to keep going when unbelievable challenges came our way? Things started to come to mind and fall into place to make more sense of why our family had faced so many tough challenges. I began to see a bigger purpose and discovered that perhaps I had been being taught something that I should one day share. Since you are reading this, I would have to say that this day has come.

So many times, I had family and friends say things like, "How do you seem to always get the big stuff?" or

"Seriously, again? Is it really happening to you guys again?"

Don't get me wrong—all along I knew we had some huge hurdles. Yet I was always able to find others who were facing challenges that I could not imagine trading places with, or even contemplate what it would be like to have to go through their challenge. I knew many people who were not as blessed as we were, yet I also knew that we had gone through more than our fair share, and I found value in knowing that there was a bigger picture. There was a reason why we had been given these tough challenges. And if we would just trust, listen, and share our experiences, it would benefit others. I wanted to find a way to believe that by sharing our stories and the lessons we learned, others could be served. They could learn new ways to handle things and discover tools that would have a bigger impact in their lives. They could learn new ways to look at things, or just learn to have a different focus. After all, perhaps all that we had gone through was not in vain, right?

As I reflected back over the years of difficulties and challenges, I was able to see how we have grown and learned from each one. Believe me, there were definitely some years in there when I could not see through it. I became victim to my circumstances, and it really cost me during that time. I paid a heavy price for those times I wallowed in disbelief and despair. I know firsthand what true depression, at its deepest core, feels like—and how debilitating it can be. I have spent sleepless nights contemplating if this life is really worth living. There were times when I wanted to give up and hide from the world, in fact, I remember a short stretch of time where I did hide. I stayed in my bedroom and thought I could shut out the world and it would get better. There was even a time when I felt everyone would be better off if I were not alive. Those were really dark times for me and for my family.

There are still times I wonder if it would have been better to go back and erase those years, or at least pretend for everyone—including myself—that they did not really exist! I have wondered if somehow people would respect me more if I continued to keep quiet, hoping that nobody ever really saw the authentic real me and my failing moments. But what I have found is that by being authentic and true, I have become more relatable. And I have been able to assist so many more people because I have been willing to put myself out there.

I know, and believe completely, that I am stronger now because of my challenges. I know how profound the pain of depression and self-hatred can be, and what kind of battles one must fight to just get through the day. It is through unwavering trust that I write this all into a book. I fully trust that it will assist others along their journey to find true happiness—through love, joy and peace.

I know deep within me, that I have gone through really tough trials to understand how a person could feel that way, or to have the feelings completely overtake them. In my pain, I knew all the right answers. I knew how I *should feel* or what I *should tell* people when they asked. I knew how to hide my true feelings and fears, and *pretend* that everything was just fine.

I was the queen of stuffing my emotions to the point that I did not cry publicly or show emotion—to the extent that I was even referred to one time as an ice queen! This was done publicly in front of over 50 people that were my peers and it was pretty tough to take. At first, it made me very angry. After all, that man had NO idea what I had gone through.

He had no idea the trials I had been going through over the past five years. I was dealing with adoption, my oldest son with a brain tumor and cancer, my daughter's head not growing and her need for head reconstruction surgery, and my husband's ATV accident and head injury. Then there was the difficulty of having a family of six, and living in a camping trailer for an entire year while building our home, because we incurred a debt in excess of $80,000 in medical bills from the past year—requiring us to sell our home and move into the RV, and my need to become the general contractor after my husband had his head injury. But what had put me over the top was the very recent and horrific suicide death of my own twin brother. How dare this man lecture me!

On the outside, it looked as if I had it all together, yet inside my head, I was a complete wreck! For a long time, I thought it was entirely my own fault. Yet what I learned, is that for many years, the stories I told myself were complete lies. I allowed my horrible self-talk and negative feelings to become my reality. These negative thoughts were not allowing the good things to even get into my head.

What I have found in my journey to get to this point is that I am not alone in the overwhelming feelings and the self-doubt. I was not surprised that others, too, had similar feelings and fear. I was amazed to discover that most people shared these same feelings on some level. I was not alone, but rather more common than not. As I have mentored hundreds of people who are also struggling in their own lives,, I have found many commonalities with them.. I have also discovered that implementation of these simple, yet profound traits, would cause immediate change in their situation, and create such a different outcome for them. I knew I had to make this available for others to easily access it, and to create a plan that could immediately improve their lives and create a substantially new focus—a way to change their lives from the Inside Out.

If you want to see significant change in your life, you must be willing to make significant changes. I have heard that a person is the result of the five people they spend the most time with in their life. Look at your own life, and ask yourself who you spend most of your time with, and if they are where you aspire to be?

Maybe it's time to "clean out some cobwebs," or even let some people in your life stop being such a priority? Maybe it is time to step up your game and spend a few more evenings out where you are able to rub shoulders with others that are where you want to be. We are all creating our own reality. We are creating our lives by the choices we make. Is it time to make some different choices?

I share these incredible 7 Traits to CHANGE YOU, Your Life, and Your World. It has been through implementation of all seven of these traits into my life, on a consistent basis, that I have been able to ultimately see light at the end of the tunnel, some days. They have even given me the ability to see a rainbow on a more difficult stormy day, and find treasure within those days when I know it is not within my control to change what is happening. I can have peace as I trudge forward with faith, knowing that I am doing my best and I am being valiant in my efforts—that I am enough.

Do you really believe that you are enough? Are you being valiant in your efforts?

When I live these 7 Traits, my life is full of happiness and joy. I am able to feel whole and complete, and know what a difference I am able to make in other people's lives. I am able to share with others what I have learned through many years of challenges and thousands of hours of education and effort. I am having a profound impact—and this is my mission.

It makes my heart happy to know that by sharing my story, other people have an opportunity to avoid some of their own pain, and are able to move forward faster. Through my sincere vulnerability and willingness to share with you my hardships, pain, and even failures, I am able to give to you a piece of hope. I desire to give you strength to continue on, to empower you to keep going, and to give you ideas of how you can do it differently—perhaps even inspire you to focus on life in completely new ways, even though none of these traits are new ideas.

As you join me, and implement these 7 Traits, your life will begin to change. Your attitude will improve. Your relationships will reach new levels. You will accept yourself and begin to trust yourself completely. You will know that you are Enough—just the way you are! You will find joy in the things all around you, and you will cherish your life at new levels. You will improve relationships with your family, and see improvement and success at work. Trust the process, and allow it to work for you. I invite you to take the steps necessary, and be open to doing things a little differently—to have All Things Possible in your life!

It takes courage to create change. It takes personal accountability and follow-through. It takes determination. It also takes believing in yourself, your brilliance, your worth and deciding that you are responsible for your future and for your happiness. Leadership is always more effective when we live the 7 Traits and we live them from the Inside Out. Our influence expands and our lives flourish as we become the Leader that we want to follow!

"It's the little things that we do on a consistent basis that will ultimately change our lives!" ~Kris Barney

TRAIT ONE:

SHOW Sincere Service

Simple Service vs Sincere Service

"It's the little things we do on a consistent basis that ultimately change our lives!"

"Everyone has the power within them to conquer any challenge life throws at them and be stronger because of it!"

"Challenges will come to all of us. How we choose to see and handle them will determine if we go through them and learn, or simply endure them."

Chapter 1 Simple Service vs Sincere Service

"The best way to find yourself is to lose yourself in the service of others." ~Mahatma Gandhi

Story: Mylar Balloon Lesson Learned

It was June 1995. My oldest son was diagnosed with a cancerous brain tumor. I had four children ages 9, 7, 5, and 11 months. My son and I spent 180 days, within a time span of 11 months, at Primary Children's Hospital. Most of my nights were spent sleeping in a wooden rocking chair. This was the most horrendous year I had ever experienced in my life, up until that point. I had gone through some pretty tough times before, but this year was unlike anything I could imagine. At the same time, I was an entrepreneur with my own business, PTA President of the Elementary School, held a leadership position in my church, and had an extremely young family. We had a lot going on!

As the months passed, I noticed my son was having a difficult time staying at the hospital. His aversion to even going was a constant struggle for both of us, and I knew I had to create something different for him. After all, he was the one who was really going through the worst year imaginable. On the way to the hospital that day, I told my son that we would be doing our hospital stays a bit differently. We were going to go to the gift shop and purchase a Mylar balloon, tie it to a Beanie Baby, and take it to our room. Then we would visit patients—yes, all the other kids who were also in the hospital—until we found the perfect person for that balloon.

My son, being almost 10 years old, thought this was an awful idea. During our conversation in the car on the way to the hospital, he even said, "That's a lame idea." Yep, my nine-and-a-half-year-old son thought I had completely lost it. And if truth be told, I am pretty sure at this point I was feeling like I had lost it too. But when we got to the hospital, we went straight to the gift shop. I told him to pick out the balloon and the little stuffed animal—at that time Beanie Babies were the craze! He, being all grown up, and a nine-and-a-half year-old BOY, decided he would outsmart me, and picked a pink congratulations balloon. PINK! This would mean we would be visiting an awful lot of girls. Do you know how often a pink congratulations balloon is used at a children's hospital? Almost never!

But we found her—she was also 9 years old. She was celebrating her last chemotherapy treatment. She was done! This was incredible. What were the odds that we would find her and that she, too, had suffered with a brain tumor and was now done with her treatment? We were completely overjoyed to find her, but we were also amazed at what this created within us. We visited a lot of kids that day in the hospital, and do you know what else we found? We found a child who would never leave the hospital alive. We found a little girl who would never walk again—she would spend the rest of her life in a wheelchair. We also met a seven-year-old little boy who was from out-of-state. He had to be in the hospital 21 days a month, and his parents could only afford to spend one long weekend with him for each hospital stay. Three to four days—that was it! Every month!

The real lesson we learned was that we did not have it so bad. When you take your focus off of yourself, it allows you to see what others are going through. Suddenly, our problems were not quite so big anymore!

We began doing this on every visit. It became our game. Everyone started knowing us as the Mylar balloon visitors. Everything about our care began to change. Suddenly, I had a chair that folded down into a bed without asking for one. We were placed in a corner suite room that was bigger, had a nice view, and was quieter and darker at night so we could sleep. Our oncology doctor, who had horrible bedside manner with children, somehow learned how to tell an occasional joke and crack a smile. Our favorite nurses were assigned to us regularly—we had friendly faces to visit and friends to go see while we were at the hospital every time we were now admitted. Our fun was putting a smile on as many faces as possible each day. And the time seemed to fly by.

Our lives were blessed each day that we spent at the hospital—even on the days that we got food poisoning, and chemo poisoning. Our trial was simply not as difficult. The lesson in this entire project was that we needed to give sincere service by taking our focus off of ourselves and finding how we could serve others.

Our lives were so blessed by serving the other children. It empowered us to keep going—even when our road was really tough. No, it did not take our trial away, but it gave us hope. It allowed us to see that others had it much worse than we did. I never imagined when we started our little game, that it would bless our lives so much. Nor did I realize the lesson I would be teaching my own children, and all the children that we served that year. I watched it change the lives of our doctors and nurses, and the other mothers at the hospital began to smile at us. Other people began to visit each other—people began serving one another because it was rubbing off on them. The staff and even the hospital leadership were noticing what was happening. It was changing everything around us. This simple act of service, done regularly, became a huge blessing in our lives, and in the lives of so many others. Our hearts were full.

When you are willing to play outside of the box with service, it actually becomes a game and is fun. It becomes something you look forward to, and can even be achieved with consistency. But most importantly, it creates fulfillment within yourself—all while going through a horrendous circumstance at the same time.

What is your 'Mylar balloon' moment? What can you do that is unique to you in serving others? How can you be remembered or leave a legacy? How do you make people feel? What is unique to you that others want more of?

Albert Einstein said; "Only a life lived in the service of others is worth living."

This is so true! Who likes to be around someone who is always complaining or always has it worse than we do?

It REALLY is not about YOU!

This can be hard to hear, and for some people hard to believe. But to have a healthy, prosperous life full of abundance—one must live in service. Completely living in service means to be Outwardly Focused. To become proficient at giving service, we must become automatic at being outwardly focused.

It is human nature to be inwardly focused. For the inwardly focused person, everything is about them. How many times have we heard the phrase, "It's not all about you," and yet this is the hallmark of an inwardly focused person.

An outwardly focused person operates from the Inside Out. It is when we train ourselves to be outwardly focused that we are the most successful! It is incredible to see the difference in co-workers, neighbors, and even family members when we come from a space of service.

Service is essential to successful living. As we bless the lives of others, we bless our own life. If we will strive to always be in service to others, our own lives will be better. It is a universal truth that what we put out into our universe, is what we are given back. It is a true principle. The more good you do and put out there—with no intent on getting anything in return, the more your own situation will prosper, and you will have success and abundance. Truth be told, what you put out into the universe, whether good or bad, will come back to you—multiplied. For no other reason than that, we should all want to put our best into the universe, like abundance, love and service. Right?

Have you been in a purchasing situation during which you felt 'sold'? How did that feel? Good or bad? Did you like it? Of course not! Nobody wants to be sold.

Have you been in a purchasing situation in which you felt served? How did that feel? Good or bad? Did you like it? Of course you did! Everyone loves being served.

Nobody wants to feel sold, yet everyone wants to feel served! So that is proof that we should be outwardly focused.

Story: Sold or Served

Many years ago my husband and I flew to Arizona to purchase a motorhome. We were ecstatic! It was just three years old, top of the line, more extravagant, and bigger than any of the motorhomes we had previously owned. As we were driving it back to Utah, we pulled into a gas station in Beaver, Utah. We watched as one of the service technicians from the shop watched us pull in and immediately came out to 'help us' fuel up our motorhome. Even though this was NOT his job, we thanked him and gave him a generous tip.

As soon as we tipped him, he began telling us that we needed shocks on our motorhome, and that we would not even make it to Salt Lake City without new ones. This was in addition to some other things which he felt were urgent items that needed repair. Keep in mind that we owned our own Mobile Mechanic Business. My husband was an ASE Certified mechanic. We KNEW we were being SOLD! We were pretty upset at how this technician was handling the situation, and even felt attacked.

During the 20 years since that situation, we have NEVER used that gas station again. It was an immediate turn off. It resulted in us deciding, "Avoid this place if at all possible!" We have spent **thousands** of dollars in fuel in Beaver since that day, because we love to play and we have to drive right through there. But none of our money was spent at that gas station. SOLD not SERVED?

What I have learned is that you cannot feel sold and served at the same time. You will always feel the one that is stronger. Being sold feels awful, it feels like we are being taken advantage of. Nobody wants to feel this way. Served, however, feels great—and even creates different chemical responses in your body. We are even healthier when we are the one serving. Interesting thought, right?

Gandhi said, "The best way to find yourself is to lose yourself in the service of others."

We found this to be so true while we were in the hospital. We wanted nothing more than to lose ourselves in the middle of that horrific nightmare. And we were able to lose ourselves as we served others from our hearts.

On a daily basis, if you will think questions like, "What can I do for you?" or "How can I be of service to this person?" You will start to 'hear' or 'think' of an answer to those specific questions. Learn to trust it and listen better—then take action on those things you are hearing or thinking, and start doing something about them. You will then be able to see it as 'intuition' or perhaps your 'natural knowing'. As you serve and do for others, your own life is blessed in ways that you cannot even imagine. For a lot of us, we have great intentions. But until they become completed actions, they are still just an unanswered wish. Taking action and actually doing the service for someone else can even be considered an answered prayer, or an answered blessing, to that person. Your heart will be touched and you will feel empowered as you serve others, fulfill your own intuition, and find your true natural knowing.

I know you have probably heard a lot about service in the past. And I'm sure most of you get involved with service on a regular basis—which is wonderful! I have always loved service. Most people will answer me in the affirmative when I ask them if they participate regularly in service. Yet most of them are doing the type of service that I consider simple service.

I have learned, and continually teach that there are two types of service: Simple Service and Sincere Service. Let me explain what I mean by placing all service in these two categories.

First is **Simple Service**: This is something that we do daily. It is expected, even required. We have signed up for this. Simple service is the kind of service that you will feel guilty if you do not do. This can also be considered obligated service. It's the service that you do out of obligation, or that you feel you are supposed to do. For example, perhaps others are watching, and it would be a good thing for you to do in order to show your employees you are doing it too. Every person does some kind of simple service.

Let me give you some other examples: you choose to be in a relationship such as marriage, which means you choose to serve that person regularly. You choose to be a parent, so you have chosen to serve that child for the rest of your life! You sign up or agree to take a community or church position, or be on a committee—it will come with service. Maybe you have accepted a job, and it comes with a considerable amount of service in working with co-workers, as well as customer service!

Simple service can feel like it is:

- Assigned

- Required
- Expected
- Obligated
- A To-Do List
- Repetitive
- Takes Effort
- Required
- Somewhat Stressful
- Guilt Driven

Second is **Sincere Service**: Sincere Service is service that you feel deep within your heart. You are changed by performing this service, and you are a better person for having done it. It raises your character. It is defined by superior service to others. It is doing something for someone else that they cannot do for themselves. It is treating a customer with excellence because it is what is best for them—it is in their best interest. It is putting our own interests or agendas aside. It is showing gratitude for your client because you genuinely do care about them. It is being genuinely happy for others' success. It is doing it anonymously and not seeking recognition for doing it. It feels good.

Sincere Service:

- Feels Good
- Gains Respect
- Creates Loyalty
- Builds Self-worth
- Creates Connection
- Moves you Forward
- Creates Abundance
- Builds Relationships
- Raises your Character
- What you put out you get back—multiplied

Isn't this what we all want?

Story: Lake Powell Boat Storage

For more than 15 years, we have had a houseboat, or a cabin cruiser boat, stored at Lake Powell in the dry storage. There are a number of companies that provide this service for boats, especially for a cabin cruiser. They store the boat safely for you when you are not there. And when you are headed down to the lake, you can just call and let them know. They will set it out of the secured area and have it ready and waiting for you, so you can hook onto it, drop it into the lake, and go play. We use the same company every year, even though they are more expensive and not as convenient. Why? Because they have superior Sincere Service!

- They know our names.
- They show us how much they care every time.
- They thank us for our business every time we are there.
- They set out our boat, plug it in, and take extra care with it.
- They know us on the phone when we call to set out the boat.
- We are a top priority to them and we know it.
- They are happy and cheerful with us.
- They honestly want us to have a wonderful vacation while we are there, and they make sure to assist us to start it off right.

This is Sincere Service! We do not care that it costs us more—it is worth it!

My question to you is this: Are you treating your family, friends, co-workers, associates, neighbors, clients, and customers so that they know you want what is in their highest good, or best interest? Is this something that is important for you? Are you continually creating ways for them to know you value them and are willing to put them first?

Here is the acronym I use to teach this concept. I train on this for several hours and there is a lot of depth to it. But for right now, I just want to share with you what it is, and a little idea for you to understand it.

SHOW Sincere Service.

S=Sacrifice: Sacrifice your time, talents, and abilities. Look for ways to serve easily. Prepare yourself to be of service.

H=Humble: It's really NOT about YOU! We must humble ourselves to be in the service of others. This gets to be a daily practice of service to everyone around you. And to do this—one needs to be humble.

O=Operate: Operate from your Heart. Do not overthink it. Too often we are in our head rather than our heart. We always do better when we come from a space of feeling.

W=Willing: Be willing to do for others—to put others first. Be willing to meet the needs of others. Be willing to get out of your comfort zone and look for ways you can embrace being service-minded. Be willing to take action on those random thoughts like: *I should call blank,* or *I should stop by and check on so and so*. Once you begin listening, and are willing to take action on your intuition, it will become stronger and you will easily know what you should do.

One of the easiest ways to up-level in this area quickly, is to ask yourself good questions every day. Learn good questions. Make a list and use them often. When you are familiar with the best questions for you, this becomes second nature. Start with something like:

1. Who can I serve today?
2. Who can I make a difference for?
3. How can I up-level my service efforts?
4. What can I do to assist someone else?
5. How can I change someone's life today?

As you focus on Sincere Service, the benefits are incredible! You will:

- Get Referrals
- Increase Sales
- Create Abundance
- Build Relationships and Connection
- Make Challenges and Trials Easier
- Gain Loyalty and Customers for Life

The KEY to Authentic Happiness is Sincere Service! Doing Sincere Service on a regular basis will give you authentic happiness—in your heart—always.

Strive to be outwardly focused. It really is not that hard. As you do, it becomes almost second nature. It becomes so easy to start to see what you can do for others—without ever being asked. Those who truly serve feel peace and joy. Even amidst their own trials. Service truly is a game changer. It is easy to do and immediately changes your life. How can you shift into Sincere Service right now to create the life you want?

If you truly want your own life to change, embrace Sincere Service!

"It's the little things we do on a consistent basis that ultimately change our lives!" ~Kris Barney

Chapter 2

What She Taught Me at Nine, Saved Me at Twenty-Nine

"Your greatest test is when you are able to bless someone else while you are going through your own storm." ~Zig Ziglar

Story: My Incredible Mother

It was early in the morning April 19, 1984. I looked out the window on this memorable day to see beautiful fluffy snowflakes falling to the ground. ***Wait! Snowing?*** *Not today!* It was my wedding day,, and in all of my dreams of an April wedding, it did not include snow! What was happening?

Growing up, all I ever wanted to be was a mother. Sure, there were some pretty great ideas of what I could be—especially for a girl who had several full ride Scholarships lined up. But deep down, I wanted a husband, children, and a family I could call my own.

I grew up in a family known as "The Brady Bunch"—our last name was Brady and we had three girls and three boys. We definitely fit the mold of the iconic 70's show. I hated being the youngest girl, because that meant I was Cindy. She was whiny and always acted like a baby—and that was definitely not me! Our home life was picture-perfect. The only thing missing was the maid named, Alice—although I always thought she would have been a great addition!

That snowy April day came at the conclusion of my year at college. I married the man of my dreams and set out to live happily ever after! Away we flew on a ten-day honeymoon, and I thought I had completely arrived! Upon returning from our honeymoon just two days later, the flooding in 1984 came through Utah County, and washed away my husband's mechanic business. We had tools floating across I-15 in a four foot wall of water! It completely buried my "Smokey & the Bandit" Trans Am car, except for the top couple inches of the fire engine red roof that you could see barely poking out above the water. That Trans Am was of course my prize possession. I had worked very hard waiting on tables at Porter's Place, and working as a manager for the pizza joint! I worked hard and paid cash for my awesome car! I loved that car with all my heart, and this was devastating! I had been married for two weeks and now my car was ruined. But that was not the most important thing going on, nor was it what we focused on saving. We were working as fast and furious as possible, sandbagging to save my in-laws' home, the mechanic shop, and the neighbors' homes around them. We worked around the clock that week, trying to save anything we could possibly save! That should have been a sign to me that things ahead might not be easy.

That was 35 years ago. Yes—we are living the "Happily Ever After" dream—but it has been an unbelievable journey to get to where we are. Not to mention the lessons that we have learned along the way.

By the time I was 24 years old, I had three boys under three-and-a-half years of age, and an emergency hysterectomy to save my life. That is what you could call a totally crazy, busy Mom! But I loved every minute of it.

Less than five years later, we were blessed, by what I call an "Angel Mother," to be given the opportunity to adopt our baby girl. Life was complete. We had four kids, and we were on top of our game. At this point in my life, I had my own business, some pretty active little boys, and a brand new baby girl who was born 10 weeks early and had medical complications.

Eleven months later, my oldest son, who was nine, was diagnosed with a brain tumor. We fought for his life—doing surgery, radiation, and chemotherapy for almost a year. We spent 180 days at the hospital in less than eleven months. Part way through that year, our baby girl's head was not growing, and she had to have a major skull reconstructive surgery. This put us in the hospital with two children, in different ICU units, fighting for life on a daily basis. As a mother, all I wanted to do was take away their pain. I wanted to make them better, and hoped I could be strong enough to handle this. We were living out this unbelievable horror story and I could not believe just how horrific it was.

Upon completion of the last chemotherapy treatment, and reaching the 120 day mark out of head surgery for my daughter, I could finally allow her to be a toddler and not have to hold her 24x7. At this point, we thought that the whole family deserved a change of scenery and could use a good vacation. We gathered our things together and went on a trip with a four wheeler club, called the Sand Seekers. We had been members of the club for some time, and headed out for St. Anthony Sand Dunes, in Idaho, to celebrate the July 4th weekend. Upon arrival to our camp, the dad's all got together to take off on what they called a "boys' ride." It was only for the adult men in the group, and it would be a hard, fast, and exciting ride through the sand dunes on their hopped up, custom built four wheelers.

A few hours later, they returned to camp with my husband tied down, strapped to his best friend, and missing his four-wheeler. He had been in a horrific ATV accident and, of course, had an extremely serious head injury! The first week, in almost a year, that we had not been in the hospital—and we were now headed to a hospital in Idaho, while on vacation! Seriously, three critical head cases in one year! This felt like too much for anyone to handle!

Due to all the time spent at the hospital and with the doctors, we now owed in excess of $80,000 for our 'share' of the medical bills. We fit in that strange category of—too rich to receive help and too poor to have the money—and as a result, we were forced to sell our home. We moved our little family into a small camping trailer, on a piece of property we were purchasing to someday build the home of our dreams. And there we stayed, while we built our new home. My husband and I were our own General Contractor in the building of our home, so naturally since my husband now had a head injury, the General Contractor position would become my responsibility.

This was an exceptionally tough time in my life! I questioned how I could ever do this! That is when I had to dig really deep, pull my 'big girl panties' all the way up, and find the courage and strength to go on. As I searched for strength, I realized how I was getting through it all. It was because of my own mother!

When I was nine years old, my mother was pregnant with her sixth child. I am a twin and we were right in the middle. At this time in my life, I had no idea what my mother was teaching me, or how it would impact my life later. She was going through a difficult complicated pregnancy, while assisting my father to build their new home—they too were the General Contractor.

During that time, my father suffered a very deep depression and was hospitalized for an extended time. My mother now had to take complete control of caring for our family, while being pregnant, chasing the hospital constantly, building the house, and going to work—yet **NEVER** ever did I hear her complain. She dug in deep, pulled those 'big girl panties' all the way up, and just handled it! She was positive and caring, never uttering an unkind thing. Never did she shirk. I watched her as she would find ways to serve others, and she always had an outward focus. She could have easily gotten overwhelmed and frustrated, yet she held huge positions in our church, was prominent in our community, and served others constantly. She worked many hours tirelessly to make sure that all five children were loved and cared for, all while supporting a husband going through a tough time. What I did not know was how much this example would play out in my life when I was faced with such similar circumstances.

What she taught me when I was nine, saved me when I was twenty-nine! Her example, her love, and her willingness to get through the tough stuff, gave me the courage and strength to carry on. Her priority to service, and finding a way to focus outwardly to bless the lives of others, seemed to come so naturally to her. Yet, I know how much she must have made it a conscious effort to do life differently. She had to make the decision to do life better and find a way to be strong. It was her conscious choice to serve others—to take her focus off of herself, and do all she could to live in gratitude and service. The entire time, she was teaching leadership qualities and instilling in me the strength to get through any challenge and still contribute to the world while going through it. She was setting an example I could follow, and live by, my entire life—no matter what!

Our example to our children, co-workers, friends and everyone within our influence, will have far greater impact than anything we ever tell them, or any gift we buy them. We are the combined results of our mothers and fathers, our leaders and teachers—all those in that village that raised us! I am so thankful and blessed to have such phenomenal parents. It is through the real life example of my mother—not her words—but her complete actions and her service, that changed my life. When I faced our son having a brain tumor, and spent those 180 days at Primary Children's Hospital, it was my mother's example that allowed me to immediately see that I had to create a way to take our focus off of ourselves and dive into a way to serve others, in order to keep my sanity! You will have a chance to read what we decided to do, which interestingly enough, was when my oldest son was nine years old, just as I was when I witnessed my own mother's example.

If you want your life to change, do service. Look outside of yourself and your circumstances enough to see that you do not have it as bad as someone else, You could serve those around you, whether they are better off or not, and make a difference. It is through Sincere Service that we can find our own way out of the dark. It is also through Sincere Service that we create that amazing community feel at work—we have the winning team in the organization, we no longer have employee retention issues, our community comes together, our family life and relationships are exceptional, and we feel happiness, love, and peace.

It was not until I actually reflected back on my own mother that I realized she had also gone through one of the roughest years I could imagine. Yet, through service to others and her children, she owned her strength and truly endured to the end of the difficulties to become a stronger and better version of herself. Isn't that what we are all striving for—the reality to become a stronger and better version of ourselves? How interesting that the more we lose ourselves in the service of others, the more we refine who we want to become.

When we can find ways to look outside of ourselves and do good for other people—to submit ourselves to Sincere Service—that is when we, not only move other people's lives forward, but we move our own life forward. It took me actually doing this to realize the importance it would play in our lives. I had always been about service, yet this raised the bar to a new level once I allowed it to burrow a way deep into my heart.

What I can tell you is that it truly is the little things that you do on a consistent basis that ultimately changes your life!

"Everyone has the power within them to conquer any challenge life throws at them, and to be stronger because of it!" ~Kris Barney

Chapter 3

What He Learned at Nine, Changed Us Forever

"You never know how strong you are, until being strong is your only choice. Cowboy Up!" ~Jesse Barney

One day, I was speaking at the "Born to Shine Conference" with an audience of mostly women. After I spoke, I was walking off the stage and back around the side of the audience, when all of the sudden a woman came up to me and said, "You have to write his story for my book!" She had been introduced to me earlier at that event, and had spoken to me about my own story and all that our family had been through. She wanted me to write and submit my story to see if the editors would choose it to go into her book. After hearing me speak from stage however, she now wanted both mine, and my son's story to be submitted.

I did write my son's story of that horrific year, from his perspective—and I even wrote my own story. It was in writing his story that I knew I had to write my own book. In fact, I am sure it will be several books that I write. But I want to share this with you for you to get a different perspective, and to allow you to see Sincere Service from the eyes of a nine year old boy.

Story: My Year of Life Lessons

In the Spring of 1995, I was living a life that all nine-year-old boys could only image in their dreams. Life was good. I was almost a foot taller than anyone else my age, which had come in extra handy during football season the previous fall. I was put on the line of scrimmage right from the first day, because of my size and ability. I played nearly the whole game every time. The coaches were already making plans for the next football season and trying to get me on their team. I loved football. The result in soccer was the same. I could kick the ball hard and most kids were a bit intimidated going up against me. I was very athletic and my size was a huge advantage. I was five-foot-two-inches tall, I wore a man's size nine shoe, and I weighed 115 pounds. The doctors said that according to the size graphs they had researched, I would be well over six-foot-six-inches tall when I stopped growing. That was not too outrageous for me, because my uncle—my mother`s twin brother—was six-foot-four-inches tall.

That spring, I was playing baseball. I learned how to pitch and practiced almost constantly. I had a pretty good arm for my age bracket because of my strength and, of course, my size. I developed a strong swing, and was able to connect with the ball every time I got up to bat. I hit home runs on a regular basis, and even hit a grand slam during our team's third game.

My family spent almost every night at the ballpark, between the baseball and T-ball games of my two younger brothers and I. I am the oldest of four kids. My two brothers were seven and five, and my sister, known as the Princess, was just 10 months old. We had just completed the soccer season in April and now it was full-on baseball time.

It was the rainiest month I had ever known. I decided that the rained-out games were not the worst thing that could happen, when I found myself very sick at the beginning of May. Four games had been called off, and I had to miss practice twice because of a fever and headaches. So mom took me to the doctor for tests. Sure enough, I had full blown strep throat. My mom was not surprised much, because she found out that twelve other kids in my school class were also out of school due to strep throat. Even my third grade teacher had been diagnosed with strep throat. After ten days on antibiotics, I was still very sick, but I lied to my mom and told her I was ok, because I wanted to play baseball. My headache was really bad, but I just couldn't stand the thought of missing another game. I had now been sick for almost three weeks, and a second trip to the Doctor had confirmed that I, indeed, still had strep throat. They changed my prescription to a stronger antibiotic, and noted that I had dropped eight pounds.

The next game was the first time that year that I had struck out. That hadn't happened yet in this whole season! It was hard to see the ball and I wasn't sure what was going on. When I tried to pitch, I was off as much as I was on, and the coach pulled me out as pitcher and said that I looked really sick. He told me to rest on the bench. Even before the game was over, my mom pulled me from the game and took me home. The next day was the last day of third grade. I was excited for summer!

Saturday I had another baseball game. I had been throwing up a little, but did not tell anyone because I did not want to miss another game. We got to the baseball park that morning and the coaches were all pretty busy getting the team ready to go, so my Mom started warming me up, getting my arm ready to pitch. She had done this with me before. We were over on the sidelines throwing the ball back and forth. After a few throws, we started throwing it harder back and forth. On the next throw, my mom really sent it to me. I prepared to catch the ball, yet I saw three of them coming at me. I missed the ball and it smacked me right between the eyes. I stumbled around for a second until my mom got to me. My nose was bleeding all over the place and I was a mess.

She asked me what happened, "Why didn't you catch the ball?"

All I could say was, "Which one? You threw three of them at me." Then I threw up again.

"That's it. We are going home," she said.

I continued to throw up the whole weekend. I could not even hold down water. My mom had been on the phone with our doctor. He prescribed anti-nausea medication and scheduled to see us first thing Monday morning.

At the Doctor's office, he examined me and we discovered I had now lost 15 pounds. He was getting concerned. The strep test was negative this time so he started looking for other reasons to explain why I was still so sick. He asked about the goose egg and black eye, so my mom told him about warming me up for my game and that I missed catching the ball. When she said that I told her I saw three baseballs coming at me, his concern grew.

He immediately tested my sight and said, "I am sending you to a Neurologist." That was the beginning of the summer of 1995—a summer that changed my life forever.

I went to the Neurologist and after the examination, he said that he thought it was just migraine headaches. But he wasn't settled with it, so he scheduled me for an MRI the next morning at 6:00 a.m. He said he would prescribe medication once he got the report from the MRI, and told us to come up to his office on the third floor of the hospital right after we got done.

The next morning, I was still throwing up and unable to hold down any food or water. They got me ready to go into the MRI machine. My mom sat right outside of the machine so that if I threw up, she could help me. I was strapped down and told not to move or they would have to start the tests over. When the tests started, there was just one lady at the computer and a nurse to give me medication through an IV. I began dry-heaving, so they pulled me out of the machine. I saw that there were now five people around the machine, besides my mom. As soon as my mom got me settled, back in I went, and the MRI machine began banging loudly again. They told me the tests would last about 20 minutes, yet it had been over an hour and I was still in there.

I could see the concern in my mom's eyes when they finally pulled me out. There were now eight people prodding and poking at me. I didn't know what was going on and they weren't letting my mom come near me. Finally, they got finished and told my mom that we were to wait in the lobby for the doctor to come down.

We walked out to the lobby, and my mom said, "The Doctor told us to come up to his office, not wait in the lobby."

We went out into the hall and as we did, the Neurologist walked up. He said, "Mrs. Barney, this is completely out of my league. The head of Neurosurgery is on his way down right now. You need to wait for him here in the lobby."

Just then, we saw a bald man running down the hall dressed in doctor scrubs. He came over to us and said, "Are you Jesse?"

I nodded and he started doing a bunch of coordination tests on me and looking into my eyes with a flashlight. Right there in the waiting room with about 40 people staring at me!

No one had told us anything yet. My mom said, "Can you tell me how long we are going to be here? I was told less than an hour. We have been here three hours now, and I have other children that I need to call and check on."

The Doctor said, "Look, Mrs. Barney, you are welcome to go anytime, but your son Jesse will not leave this hospital without brain surgery. He is on the schedule for tomorrow!"

WHAT THE HECK!! I thought. What did he just say? The gasp from the other 40 people in the waiting area reassured me that this was bad! I looked at my mom, and I could see, from the look on her face, that no one had told her this news either.

The doctor looked at my mother and said, "Hasn't anyone told you?"

She took ahold of my hand, looked him in the eyes and said, "No. We were only told to wait here for the doctor to come down and talk with us."

He apologized and said, "It is critical that I assess your son. He has a brain tumor the size if a lemon and so much fluid on the brain, he should not be alive! This could be a matter of life and death."

My mom put her arm around me, smiled at me, and with a straight face, looked at the doctor and said, "You go ahead and do your assessment. I need to make a couple of phone calls."

The doctor went back to testing me while my mom reached up and got the phone off the wall. Then I heard my mom's voice crack as she said over the phone, "Mom, can you go to my house? Jesse has a brain tumor, and we are being admitted to the hospital for brain surgery."

The next call was to locate my dad, who had gone to work up the canyon, and would need someone from the shop to go get him. A short time later, I heard the doctors talking to my mom saying, "He has so much water on the brain that he should not be alive. Do not let him fall asleep. We are opening up a bed in the ICU for him as quickly as possible!"

I went straight to the ICU and was put in a bed. Life as I knew it, would not be the same.

I remember the doctor telling me that because of where the tumor was, I would know my times tables in my head, and once they taught me to swallow and then speak again, I could tell them all of my times tables. The next part the doctor said was tough to take, as if the last part were not overwhelming enough—I definitely would not be able to play sports again in my life. Even best case scenario—sports were out.

I had less than a 50 percent chance of surviving the surgery, which my parents decided not to tell me, before I went under the knife for a grueling 11 hour surgery. I remember coming out of the operating room and, as they rounded the corner with my bed to take me back to the ICU unit from recovery, my parents were standing there. They were telling me how much they loved me and how great I was doing.

All of the sudden I said, "I think I am going to throw up."

My mom thrust her hands out to catch it. And tears streamed down both of their faces as she said, "He talked, he talked! He knows what's going on!" This was a good sign that all had gone well with surgery.

The next several weeks were very difficult. I could not even sit up for almost three full weeks. I had to go from lying flat, to moving my body at slight angles, in order to get the pressure in my head under control, and to also get the fluid on my brain to drain. I had two drain tubes in my head that were later removed. After almost five weeks, I was able to leave the hospital and go home. I arrived at home with my parents, to hundreds of yellow ribbons tied all over the trees in our yard, and a huge "Welcome Home Jesse" banner.

The brain tumor was malignant—which meant cancer—so I was required to do radiation and chemotherapy treatments. Radiation began the week after I got out of the hospital. It was five days a week, for six weeks, which was seriously the hardest six weeks of my life, up to that point. It made me horrifically sick, and all of my hair fell out. I had no idea I would have side effects—from them radiating my brain—for years and years to come. Chemotherapy started before they were even finished with the radiation. I was so sick from both of the treatments that I lost an additional 42 pounds, which made a total of 57 pounds lost . Being five-foot-two inches tall, and only 58 pounds now, I fit into my baby sister's umbrella stroller—except for my long legs and huge feet. Due to the fact that I could not hold down food at all, and I continued to lose weight, the doctors required me to go onto a feeding tube. This tube was taped to my face, went up my nose, down my throat, and into my stomach. For the next six months, I would have to be hooked up to a machine for 12 hours a day to allow it to feed me enough "Ensure" to keep me alive.

I had a PICC line IV placed in my arm because I was so dehydrated and sick that they could not get a regular IV into my arms, or even my legs and feet, without collapsing the veins. This line was placed so that they could take blood for tests, and also send fluids and chemotherapy drugs through that line. This line would become my friend for the next nine months. The chemotherapy poisoned the muscles in my legs, and I was required to walk with braces on both legs so that my feet would stay in position. I was told that I would have to have these braces on my legs for my entire life. I was almost completely unable to walk for about two months while these muscles tried to repair themselves. It took everything I could do to even get to the bathroom just down the hall. My mom got really good at giving me piggy-back rides, as that was the easiest way to get me from one place to another—especially when we went into the hospital.

In just over eleven months, we had spent 180 days in the hospital. It did not take long before this nine-year-old boy had enough of that. My parents told me that I never even once said, "Why me?" or complained about how horrible this year of my life was. Our family had always been about service. And even during this incredibly difficult year, we were still finding ways to look outside our own circumstances and do good for others. After completing radiation, and then starting chemotherapy, there were many days spent in the hospital. I didn't necessarily complain, but I was not happy to go. I know this weighed on my parents a lot. They knew I wanted to be like all the other fourth grade boys, playing ball, going to school, having fun, instead of being in the hospital.

On our way to the hospital in late October, my mom said to me, "Jesse, today we are going to do things differently when we get to the hospital."

"What do you mean?" I said.

"We are going to go to the gift shop, first thing, and buy a balloon," she replied.

Being a bit confused, I said, "Why?"

"Because we need to find which patient it belongs to," she said.

I looked at her a little bewildered and said, "That is lame."

My mom and dad were always coming up with crazy things like this, so I decided I would show her. We got to the hospital and walked into the gift shop. My mom said, "Well, Jesse, which one is it?"

I had been making a plan in my head and now it was execution time. "This one," I said, pointing to a pink 'Congratulations' balloon. YES, PINK!

My mom let out a laugh and asked me, "Are you sure?"

With all the confidence in the world, at least all that a nine-year-old boy has, I said, "Oh yes, I am positive!" After all, this would get her to back down off her great idea when her plan did not work, right?

It took a ton of visits that day in order to find the balloon's owner. We visited all kinds of sick kids at the hospital. It is not easy to find someone who deserves a pink 'Congratulations' balloon in a children's hospital. Guess my plan kind of backfired on me.

But—we found her. She was nine years old too. She was also diagnosed with a brain tumor. She was getting her last chemotherapy treatment that day. She was celebrating and having a party!

This was actually a great experience for me. We were doing a small act of service that day—yet I learned a ***huge truth****. When I focused on others, and concentrated on cheering them up, my own trials did not feel so heavy.*

As we visited other kids, we found one that would not leave the hospital alive, ever again. We found one that would have to spend the rest of her life in a wheelchair. We found one that was back for the third diagnosis of cancer, and would not win this battle. He became like a hero to me. He was positive and happy almost all the time. When he died, he was buried in Karl Malone's basketball uniform. I felt so sad when he died, yet I felt unbelievably lucky to have known him. Without doing our little mylar balloon game, I would never have met him. I would not have learned from him, and it would not have given me the opportunity to live my life more like him.

There was another kid that really stuck out for me that day. It was a boy who had to spend 21 days a month in the hospital. He was from out of state, so his parents could only come and spend time with him three or four days a month. They could only afford plane tickets and time off work for one long weekend. That little guy was just seven years old. The same age as my little brother! He was one that we visited every time we were in the hospital after that day. We made a special effort to spend time with him, play Nintendo, and watch movies together.

I had people with me always. It was usually my mom, because my dad was working tons of hours. Most weeks, my dad was putting in around 80 hours, doing everything he could do to stay ahead of the medical bills, and take care of our family. The rest of the time, he was home taking care of my brothers and sister.

What I learned from this little game of buying a Mylar balloon and going to visit other sick kids at the hospital, was profound. It taught me to look beyond myself, to become outwardly focused. When I stopped looking at how bad things were for me, and instead focused on what I could do to cheer up someone else, my burdens seemed lighter. I learned that a lot of kids had it worse off than I did. I had it rough, for sure, but I had support. I had a chance to survive and live a pretty normal life when I got through. I also learned that gratitude played a huge part in my recovery, as well as in keeping a good attitude. I learned that being in service to others is key. Our balloon buying and placing ritual, became something that we looked forward to. Our days spent in the hospital went by much faster. We spent those days visiting others while I was feeling good enough, and had not yet started into the throwing up stage that always came when I received chemotherapy.

My focus changed. My reality changed. My life was blessed by being able to be of service to others. Even before that year with cancer, our family had always done a huge Sub-for-Santa project. We always kept it a secret, but we were the 'Real' Santa. Each year, my dad would be a 'helper' for Santa. Every night during the Christmas season, he would go out to do Christmas parties, all dressed up in his red suit, to earn money so that we could buy Christmas for families that were having a bad year. We loved doing this every year as a family!

This Christmas was a little different. I remember many people telling my parents that they should keep the money to help pay the medical bills. But that is not what we did. I had been in the hospital a ton that December, so it was next to impossible to do all of the things necessary to buy Christmas & deliver it Christmas Eve for other families. As a family we talked about it, and decided that we were going to be the "Real Santa" to Primary Children's Hospital.

I was a 10-year-old boy the Christmas of 1995., and Nintendo was HUGE. As I remember, it was the big year for Super Nintendo! In all of Primary Children's Hospital, there were only four TV & Nintendo systems that they could bring to your room for you to use, and they had very few games to choose from. You would have to sign up on a list to check out the system, and then wait FOREVER for your turn to have it for two hours. When your two hours would come up, you would just hope and pray that your doctor did not come by to chat, or that you would have to go have other test runs and blood draws. It was like fighting, or pulling teeth, to get to have one of the systems and play games for a while—allowing us to almost forget that we were NOT living a normal life like all of our friends.

Living this battle every week is how we came up with our Grand Plan. My dad played Santa every night, and his parties all found out what we were doing that year with the money. Most of them donated double what they had paid him before so that we could have a big budget to spend. My mom worked with RC Willey, and they gave us incredible deals on the TV's, VCR's and Nintendo and Super Nintendo Systems, to support our cause. Mom also went to work getting deals on videos and games for the new systems.

On Christmas Eve, my whole family, and our best friends in the whole world, got to all dress up as Elves to go with Santa from room to room at the hospital. We got to wish all the kids a Merry Christmas and hand out the donations that had been given to the hospital. Each child got a blanket, a toy, a gingerbread house and a stuffed animal. I got to wear the green elf costume. My brothers and our friends got to push me in a wheelchair since I could not walk on my own.

I got to go into every room with Santa and see the look on every child's face that year. I knew some of them from doing our balloon game with my mom. After we had gone to all the rooms at the hospital, we got to deliver the Christmas we were able to buy—four new systems, complete with a big TV, VCR, and Super

Nintendo system, and at least six new games with each system. We were also able to purchase 60 new videos and add them to the video library so that the patients would have a chance to see the newest movies out! It was Amazing! Our hospital stays were never the same after that, because now I could get a TV & game system every time I went.

That was a night that forever changed me. It made me want to see the happiness in the eyes of children every Christmas. I got to assist our family every year with the Sub-for-Santa project, and I loved it. In November 2011, I asked the real Santa, my dad, if he would allow me to take over the tradition of being a Real Santa. I received my complete Santa Suit for Christmas that year. Of course it was early, as there is a lot of work to do for the Real Santa. Now I go out almost every night in December, as a helper, to earn money so that I can contribute in a big way to our Sub-for-Santa family project. Yes it is a ton of hours, yes it is tiring and even at times stressful. But what I can tell you is that I get to look in the eyes of children and see the happiness in their faces. I get to serve others in a remarkable way. I get to look outside of myself and then my challenges do not seem so bad after all.

My year with Cancer as a young boy, was a tough year in my life, to say the least. But what I learned and implemented in my life on a daily basis is what has gotten me through the rest of my life. I enjoy serving others and I live each day in gratitude, because I know how much this makes a difference. I lived life pretty normal for the next 16 years. Sure I had "stuff" that stayed with me from radiation and chemotherapy. In fact, I even had a few tough years in high school. But the true test for me began on Labor Day 2011, when I broke my back in a motorcycle crash and then was diagnosed with a brain tumor just 12 weeks later. I went through three brain tumor removal surgeries in just five months, because it kept growing back every eight weeks or so, plus I had to do radiation as well. That was my toughest year yet. But that is a story for another day.

What I can tell you is that I made it through because of the lessons I learned as a nine-year-old boy with cancer.

"Sincere Service is looking outside of yourself. Becoming outwardly focused on a daily basis. It is also about doing service for others every day—even when you are going through harder trials than they are. Above all, 'Genuine Gratitude' is being grateful for everything in your life, even the trials. For in them, you will learn lessons and become a stronger you."

I am sure that you can see I have been incredibly blessed to have the opportunity to be Jesse's mother. You can also see that by taking our eyes off of our misery, our challenges, and ourselves, we were able to find joy in the little things. We found true happiness with what we were doing, and we were able to create a different reality than that of a miserable eleven months of fighting for our lives.

Finding ways to serve is easy. There are opportunities everywhere if you are willing to look. Service can be as easy as visiting someone who is sick, or having a tough time. It can be feeding the homeless or helping out a coworker. It can be bringing an extra cup of coffee to work for your boss. It doesn't have to look a certain way. Just make it a focus and soon it will become a habit that comes naturally.

If you want your life to change, do more Sincere Service.

"Challenges will come to all of us. How we choose to see and handle them will determine if we go through them and learn, or simply endure them." ~Kris Barney

TRAIT TWO:

GROW in Genuine Gratitude

Generic Gratitude vs Genuine Gratitude

"Gratitude is the Ultimate Magnifier. to Change Your Life Immediately, Focus on Being Grateful."

"Fear can stop you or propel you…the choice is yours."
"Freedom is the opportunity to Be More than you were before, to Have more and to Become More. It is the Absence of Fear…True Freedom comes from Within."

"Empathy and Gratitude allow us to go Beyond Being just Compassionate and Thankful. They allow us to build Trust, Honor and Respect."

Chapter 4

Generic Gratitude vs Genuine Gratitude

"Gratitude and complaining cannot co-exist simultaneously; you must choose the ONE that best serves you!" ~Hal Elrod

I am sure you have heard, "What we are grateful for, we get more of."

That is absolutely true! What you are grateful for and show gratitude for will be multiplied and magnified. When you focus on being grateful for blessings, you will have more blessings.

It is not happiness that brings us gratitude—it is gratitude that brings us happiness! The important key is to always play huge with gratitude. Never play small with this.

I love the saying from Hal Elrod:

"Gratitude and complaining cannot co-exist simultaneously; you must choose the ONE that best serves you!"

Let me repeat that: "Gratitude and complaining cannot co-exist simultaneously; you must choose the ONE that best serves you!" Are you grateful for the things you have, or do you find yourself complaining about the things you both have or don't have? So often we can find ourselves wanting that new car or a new toy, yet we are never satisfied once we get it. Did it change everything in your world? Maybe it did—for a period of time. But to truly have gratitude around the things that we have, the unbelievable blessings that surround us, allows us to be content and fulfilled. We are not looking for that constant upgrade or the latest greatest next thing.

Don't get me wrong—I am the first person to want you to continue in this life going for the upgrade in yourself. Continue on the journey of empowerment, leadership, influence—and just plain and simple, your personal upgrade. But what I have found, is that we can easily find ourselves complaining when things are not necessarily going our way. Or when the real life challenges begin to overwhelm us—we tend to turn into the complainer. Pretty soon it gets out of control, and we find ourselves unhappy and frustrated. This is when we begin to feel unsatisfied with our clothing, our TV, or our cell phone. We begin feeling like what we have is no longer working, and we start complaining about it. We tell ourselves that we know we will be happier if we go get the upgrade. Make sure that you are not falling victim to this trap. You cannot ever create true happiness with things. You can be very happy and content with the things you already have, and their quirks, when you are filled with gratitude and are thankful for them.

"Gratitude is the Ultimate Magnifier. To Change Your Life Immediately, Focus on Being Grateful." ~Kris Barney

Our lives are always changing, and we are forever faced with daily decisions as to how we act, what we say to others, and how we feel about ourselves. If you want to change your life, and want to see immediate results, focus on gratitude. Gratitude is the ultimate magnifier. What we focus on expands and then returns to us—it's magnified. So, what are you focusing on? What do you find yourself thinking about, or even daydreaming about? Is it what is going great in your life—or what is not so great? What would happen if you were to shift just that focus, and allow yourself to see what could happen if you just did this differently? Even if you feel like you are pretty grateful and that you are not doing too badly in this area, what 'could be' if you were to 'up' your game?

Here is a question for you to consider: what is the cost, to be in a relationship with you? Are you continually adding to the bank account of positivity, or are you taking from that account and creating a negative balance in the relationship, through your negativity and complaining?

Story: The Cost of Friendship

For many years, before I knew just how important this was and created a new reality for myself, I could be found complaining. It can be easy to fall into this type of pattern. For a lot of that time, I knew no difference. It was just part of life. Everyone around me did it, and I could be found doing it too. I found friends that really 'got me' and when things were not going my way, or they were perhaps very difficult, I would be found complaining to those friends. Now at the time, I thought I was only saving my complaining for the best of the best—those who I considered to be my BEST friends. That was my best girl friend, and my husband.

Guess what happened? It caused a huge problem!

This lesson came to me with painful consequences. First of all, it is never better in a marriage when there is consistent complaining. This was not creating the kind of marriage that I wanted. In my own little mind, any time that my husband did not agree with my complaining, I would think things like, "Well, you just do not get it." or, "You had to be there…" Sound familiar? So I was extremely smart at this, and I decided not to complain to my husband because "he didn't get it anyway." And I began to mostly complain to my best friend at the time.

She was one of the best friends I had ever had, not counting my hubby, of course. We spent a lot of time together—she was the epitome of a fantastic friend. I could tell her anything—and often did. I was going through the toughest time of my life, and had been through a horrific five years of tough trials, and had actually handled them pretty well to this point. But when this last trial hit, it was the icing on the cake. I had already been assisting my cousin due to her cancer—she and I were closer than my own sisters. She was in a battle with cancer, and it had gone on for a couple years at this point. I was going over to her house and helping her out several times a week, driving her to appointments, and generally taking care of her needs. This was a four year battle with cancer that she did not win. My cousin meant the world to me and losing her was like losing a sister. But the biggest challenge for me came when my twin brother committed suicide, leaving a wife and 4 children, when we were just 33 years old. It was unbelievable to lose both of them to such tragedies—and I was spiraling out of control.

During this unbelievable tough time, I did not know how I would go on. My best friend was there with me when we got the dreaded phone call about my twin brothers death, and she immediately took over my life, handling all that needed to be handled, and being there for anything I needed. I began to struggle with depression, and complaining became second nature. After all, what did I have to look forward to anyway? Right?

Within about a two year time span, I had six close family deaths: my mother-in-law, my cousin, my twin brother, a friend, and both of my grandparents. Honestly, I really felt I was losing my mind. Yet, it did not matter. I became that person that complained more than I found gratitude. I became that person that I never wanted to be. I became that person that I, myself, despised. Through it all, I had my stalwart friend, who I turned to often, and dumped my baggage on—a lot.

Towards the end of that two years, my best friend began avoiding me. She didn't answer my calls, and things were not the same. When we finally had the conversation about what was going on, it came down to this: I was too negative. All I seemed to do was complain, and it had become too hard to be around me so much. I was CRUSHED! I cannot even explain the pain and anguish that I felt. My world had been pulled out from under me, and I had lost so much. I could not comprehend losing my best friend too! This was too high a cost. How could I go on?

What I can tell you is that this was a valuable lesson for me. It took me losing what was nearest and dearest in my heart, to see what pain I was causing. It was the hardest thing I could imagine. And yes, it made me very cautious to put myself out there with other relationships, yet it put me on the journey that I have traveled to becoming a different person. It made me want to be better and never ever be a burden to others. It created a lesson for me that I would not have learned from anyone else with the same parameters. It had a huge cost—and came with some huge regret. But I know that this was part of my journey to become someone who could reach others during difficult trials—and make a difference. It taught me just how much I had lost myself, and had become someone I never wanted to be. I went into the depths of despair and depression that I was not sure I would come out of. I had thoughts that I actually could make sense as to how my brother did what he did in taking his own life. I struggled to see that I had any value at all. There were times that I spiraled out of control.

Yet, now I am strong and assist others to overcome those same challenges. I see this whole situation from new eyes. I choose to see it in gratitude and I have chosen to learn from this valuable lesson. I have embraced it with enough belief in the value of the experience, to be grateful for this powerful lesson, and to value that my friend loved me enough to do the hard thing and be my teacher. This was tough love at its finest hour! I know for her it was not an easy choice. This was not something that she took lightly, and it weighed heavily upon her heart. This took strength and conviction, with a trust that it was for both of our own good. It perhaps even was the turning point for me to save my own life, and to fight the tough fight. For this I am truly Grateful. Even now, after many years, we remain the best of friends.

Our lives are always changing. And we are forever faced with daily decisions on how we act, what we say to others, and how we feel about ourselves. If you want to change your life, and you want to see immediate results, focus on Gratitude!

Let's talk about **Generic Gratitude**. It is gratitude for everything temporal in our lives. This encompasses the simple things, such as a roof over our head, food to eat, clothing to wear, a good job, and... shoes. We have to be grateful for shoes, right? Generic gratitude is easy and often gets taken for granted. Once we begin taking those things for granted, we are on that slippery slope of being more negative than positive. And I suggest if you are there, check to see if you are caught up in being a pretty good complainer—because they go hand in hand!

It is extremely important that we have generic gratitude. It becomes very easy to get complacent and simply overlook valuable things, like our bodies functioning and our eyesight, or our relationships and our families that we value so much! All the things that allow us to have incredible lives matter! This is not the part of gratitude that should be taken lightly. As I work with clients, more often than not, this area gets overlooked. They have stopped recognizing the value of the little things, and therefore it slips from their focus and they begin to take it all for granted. Do you appreciate being taken for granted? I am going to guess that you do not. Nobody likes being taken for granted, and neither do all the amazing things in your life! Remember, what we focus on EXPANDS. Focus on all you have to be grateful for and watch it expand, and come back to you.

Now let's talk about **Genuine Gratitude**. This one is not quite so easy, yet it will change your world if you can master it! The ultimate game changer is being grateful for literally everything in our life. This means the trials, the challenges, and even the hardships. When we can see the lessons in what we are going through, and how we created the things that happen in our lives, not only will we be able to overcome the challenge faster, but our lives will make more sense—and what we learn from it will have more value. We will become more successful in all areas of our lives.

"Gratitude is the single most important ingredient to living a successful and fulfilling life." ~Jack Canfield

Many times we find ourselves in the middle of a challenge, and we want to place blame and point fingers at whose fault it is and why it happened. But have you stopped to look at it from a different space—the space of 'what am I learning,' or 'what is this teaching me so that I can learn it faster and get through it quicker?' When we make this shift in our life, we are able to push through things so much easier. For example, remember the story about my son's cancer and how, as we took our focus off of ourselves and began focusing on how we could make a difference, it shifted how we reacted to everything that was going on. It did not make us healthier or have less medical complications—it changed how we dealt with them. The same thing is true here. When you can step back and see the view differently, it allows you to have the insight to grasp it differently and see what you are learning. Genuine Gratitude will do this for you. It will create a way in you to see it differently and actually move you forward faster. It will not take away your problems, but rather allow you to see solutions for those situations and give you the sense of well-being and strength to deal with them better.

Having gratitude for our challenges is not always easy, but this is a vital step in making a challenge lighter. You can feel gratitude for what you are learning and for the ways in which you are becoming a better person for having gone through a trial or difficulty. Often we gain strength and courage during our toughest challenges. If we will view our challenges from a perspective of gratitude, we learn things faster and experience more peace and happiness while going through the challenges.

Here is the acronym I teach about Gratitude:

GROW in Genuine Gratitude:

G=Goodness: Find the greater good. Get good at giving and receiving. Be generous. Goodness comes from your heart. This becomes second nature. So how is this done easily?

- Focus on what you have, not on what you do not have.
- Focus on what is working, not on what is not working.
- Focus on being grateful, not on being ungrateful.
- Focus on how you can serve others, not how others can serve you.

R=Ready: Be Ready to show and find the goodness. Be Ready and responsible with being grateful. Be Ready to express it often. When we express our gratitude, it shows appreciation. When we are Ready, we are living this. Be Ready to do your life differently with Genuine Gratitude as your focus.

O=Open: Be Open and willing to see things differently, striving to find the good. Be Open to look beyond the difficulties or bad situations. Oprah Winfrey said this: "What you focus on expands, and when you focus on the goodness in your life, you create more of it. Opportunities, relationships, even money flowed my way when I learned to be grateful no matter what happened in my life." I love that not only do we hear this from real people, but from famous successful ones too......Focus on Gratitude and your life will change. Thus making it a GAME CHANGER!!

W=Written: Keep a Gratitude journal. Write thank-you cards, e-mails, and give outside recognition. I have LOVED having a Gratitude Journal. I have seen significant changes in my life by having one, and using it consistently.

Gratitude is the Key to Abundance! If you want more abundance in your life, find your Gratitude.

Embrace Gratitude with every part of yourself. When you are willing to have an Attitude of Gratitude in everything you do, before you know it—things will be dramatically different.

A good way to check yourself and see how you are doing in this area is to check your attitude. When things are going smoothly, and we are filled with gratitude, our attitude is amazing. Attitudes are contagious. Have you ever been around someone with a bad attitude? Did it immediately make you happy and excited to be around that person, or were you desperate to get away from them? Let's face it—nobody wants to be around the Grumpy Grouch, Negative Nellie, or Connie Complainer. In fact, you will find that most people will avoid the person with a bad attitude at any cost. That person will have difficulty finding and keeping friends or even clients, will rarely be referred or receive positive feedback, and will usually walk around with a chip on their shoulder not even recognizing that they are creating their own situation. And sadly, they will come across jealous of the person with that fantastic personality, tons of friends, and success coming from all areas in their life.

My question for you is this: "Is your attitude worth catching?" Let's think about that. Are people attracted to you and do you have an abundance of friends and clients that are thrilled to be with you? Take a good look at your attitude as well as your results. They are important, and will give you feedback for you to take a reality check and see where you can make some adjustments. Even small adjustments create massive change over time. Again, I remind you what Hal Elrod said, "Gratitude and Complaining cannot co-exist simultaneously; you must choose the ONE that best serves you!" We are always making that choice. You are making your own decisions every day. Nobody can tick you off if you do not let them. You are the only one in complete control of YOU. You are already choosing the one that is best serving you, what are your results?

We should live each day in Gratitude. As we do, our lives are blessed and we have abundance in all areas of our lives. We get to actually see those blessings of Gratitude in our lives, as we make it our focus. Our lives can be filled with abundance if we choose to be in Gratitude. As we recognize the thousands of things that we have going right for us, at any moment, it can be incredible. But when we focus on the things that may be going wrong in our world, pretty soon, all we see and can focus on is just how awful our life is, and how we have it so hard.

3 Things you can do daily to Raise Your Gratitude:

- Gratitude Journal. Write 5x5. (5 things you are grateful for daily, at least five days a week.)
- Get Outside in Nature—Fresh air and grounding. Experience the beauty of our world.
- Focus on the positives in your life. Compliment others and yourself, give thank-you cards, and be in an accomplishment mentality. Make a list of your accomplishments daily.

Having and showing Gratitude will give you unbelievable freedom! It is amazing how just creating a daily focus on Gratitude will set you free!

"Gratitude is the Ultimate Magnifier. To Change Your Life Immediately, Focus on Being Grateful." ~Kris Barney

Chapter 5

Her Death Opened My Eyes

"As we express our gratitude, we must never forget that the highest appreciation is not to utter words, but to live them."
~John F. Kennedy

Imagine one of your greatest heroes. Who is this for you? Is it a child, a parent, a sibling, a teacher, a coworker, a neighbor, a friend, a well-known or even quite famous person? Who is this for you? I want you to really think of this person. Why are they your hero? What characteristics and traits do you admire about them and why? Do those traits draw you in and make you want to be a better person? How do they live their life?

Story: Sisters by Choice

Janet and I were first cousins. She was seven years older than I was, so growing up we were never very close. When I got married, we moved into the same city and lived fairly close to one another. We instantly became closer than ever, and even called ourselves 'sisters by choice'. Our husbands got along great and the four of us became thick as thieves. We vacationed together and even 'hung out' and had parties together every few days. For years, we raised our families together and came up with shenanigans that could not be topped. We had fun together—whether we were working or playing. We were spontaneous, creative, and living the dream.

I never really thought of her as my hero. We were really just best friends. That is until I watched her go through one of the roughest battles with cancer that I have ever seen. Keep in mind that this was not my first up close and personal experience with cancer. I had faced this little demon before— it is very up close and personal when it attacks your child! Sadly enough, she did not win this battle.

I loved her so much. We spent tons of time together. She was only 40 years old when her battle took over. She started out with what she thought was a root canal surgery. That is when they found she had a very large tumor, and was required to undergo a major surgery, removing the roof of her mouth and part of her cheek bone. The recovery was horrific and changed everything in her life. But, she was a trouper. Never a complaint!

She always made you feel better by having been around her. As she recovered from the first part of her cancer, and had gotten life more under control and a bit more normal, they found cancer in her lungs. Another huge surgery took out big sections of both lungs. She then did chemo and radiation again, and lost all of her hair and a lot of weight—she had become very thin. She could no longer eat the kind of foods that she loved, and even her speech made it hard to understand her. But as I would go over to help her several times a week, she was always in gratitude. She was grateful for everything in her life, even the simplest of things. Even when her life was horrible!

As if she hadn't been through enough, they subsequently found brain tumors—just months later, which led to more surgery. Her cancer was everywhere. The daily struggles just to survive were unreal. There became a time when she could no longer walk without help, or care for herself without assistance. She and I learned how to do a little shuffle dance across the floor to get from one place to another. Really, this was just to go the distance it took to make it to the bathroom. It would zap every ounce of energy out of her for the next few hours. Yet, she still was in gratitude. No complaining and feeling sorry for herself, every day of her life she found the good—and poured out gratitude everywhere. Even in her most difficult times, she brought laughter and happiness.

At a family party, just a few days before she passed away, she let all her nieces and nephews, along with her kids and their friends, color on her bald head while at a big party. They laughed and carried on. Everyone at the party was having fun and laughing uncontrollably. She was the center of attention and the life of this party. It was only after the party was over that she realized they had used permanent markers. She was buried a few days later with her new permanent marker tattoos on her head.

What an example she was to me. I had the privilege and honor of being able to be of service to her on an almost daily basis the last two years of her life, yet it was I who was served. It was I who was taught. It was I who learned. Was she my Sister? Yes. Friend? Yes. Incredible example? Yes. Hero? Absolutely!

"As we express our gratitude, we must never forget that the highest appreciation is not to utter words, but to live them." ~John F. Kennedy.

She did not EVER just utter words. She LIVED in gratitude to the point that even on her darkest days, people were drawn to her. She lived life to the fullest until the very end. This made it easier on everyone. Are you living each day in gratitude?

Think about it, if she would have been negative and self-centered and miserable, what legacy would she have left for her three teenage children? If she was awful to be around and acted all needy, would I have been so willing to put my own life on hold to go serve her? I would hope that I could say I would, but it would have been a much tougher decision, right?

How are you showing up on your darkest of days? When things are tough at work, do you take it out on your precious loved ones? Would you allow everyone at the party to have the time of their life drawing permanent marker tattoos on your bald head? Or would you have kept your wig on, and sat in the corner feeling sorry for yourself, just days before you died? This was the last time almost everyone in the room was able to talk with her. It was the last time she ate solid food. It was the last time all of her nieces and nephews ever saw her. What memory did she leave for them?

Our opportunity to influence or inspire others is constantly there. Our opportunity to leave a negative impression is there too. Which one will you choose?

This experience made me really take a look at life and the value I learned in this lesson. There was a huge Gift in this Garbage! I had the opportunity to see firsthand how different it could be, and how the way she lived, and courageously died, could empower everyone else—even when it was heavy and hard to bear the burden. I had lived a similar situation with my son, and had rallied to be everything I could be for him—to strengthen and build him up. But I had not look deep into the depths of this and had my eyes opened up to the magnitude of what a difference it would make for everyone else. It made an impact that was surreal and far reaching. I know that it also impacted her. It gave her strength beyond her own during those times that she felt like she could no longer fight the fight she was in. It buoyed her up when she received the bad news, over and over, and it gave her strength to be the best Mother, Wife, and Friend—even until the end.

“When you are Grateful, fear disappears and abundance appears.” ~Tony Robbins

Fear is out there everywhere in our world. It shows up in all different way,s and for each person it shows up differently and has different symptoms. Yet the results and effects are the same. It can stop you.

“Fear can stop you or propel you…the choice is yours.” ~Kris Barney

Gratitude has such a powerful impact on how fear affects us. We will face fear differently, if we are willing to live in gratitude. When we embrace gratitude, the doors of abundance are open and flowing our way. Think of the incredible things you can create by just being open to the benefits of gratitude.

My recommendation for you is this: If you are not playing huge with your gratitude, change it. If you are not spending time writing and acknowledging how grateful you are, change it. If you are allowing yourself to complain, be negative, and be self-centered, change it. It is not worth the price you are paying. This is something that is easy to change. It's FREE of charge and comes with payouts and incredible dividends.

The time is now. Up level your life, regardless of where you are at. Find the freedom you deserve and create the life you love! You will be happy you did.

"Freedom is the opportunity to Be More than you were before, to Have More, and to Become More. It is the Absence of Fear...True Freedom comes from Within." ~Kris Barney

Chapter 6

Empathy and Gratitude in the Workplace

"Gratitude is the single most important ingredient to living a successful and fulfilling life." ~Jack Canfield

I agree with Jack Canfield that the single most important ingredient to living a successful and fulfilling life is gratitude. I have watched this over and over, hundreds of times, with many different clients. It will change your entire world if you will embrace it. Allow it to become part of who you are, and watch how life changes for the good.

"I don't have to chase extraordinary moments to find happiness—it's right in front of me if I'm paying attention and practicing gratitude." ~Brene Brown

Let's talk a bit about how this plays out in the workplace. I have had clients that felt that gratitude was great advice for home, but what about work? They felt like it did not have the same value as it might have in the home. What I can assuredly tell you is that Gratitude and Empathy are HUGE in the workplace.

Think about when you are at work, whatever it is that you do—is it easier to work with people who are grateful for your assistance, value what you bring to the table, and are thankful that you are on their team? Let's look at the flip side of this. How do you like working with a complainer, or a negative moody person? Does it make your day drag and seem like it goes on forever? Usually, someone who does not embrace gratitude is the one finding fault with the project, missing deadlines, and creating issues between departments. They also tend to use a lot of blame and are less likely to give good input or feedback. Does this sound like anyone you have had the opportunity to work with?

It is difficult to work with negative people, and it is a struggle to have the desire to continue working with a company, or being a part of a team that they are also a part of. Seriously, in our world right now, there are some huge issues with employee retention, creating community in the workplace, as well as the effectiveness and productivity of the employee. We are seeing it on all sides, and in reality, for the first time ever—management levels and executive teams are expected to have raised levels of gratitude and empathy. This has become a huge need in Corporate America.

Let's face it—empathy and gratitude are really just phenomenal characteristics that we should be embracing anyway.

We have talked a ton about gratitude, but what is the hype about empathy?

Empathy is the ability to experience and relate to the thoughts, emotions, or experiences of others. Empathy is more than just sympathy, which is being able to understand and support others with compassion and with sensitivity. It is the action of understanding and being aware of, or sensitive to, and experiencing the feelings, thoughts or emotions of others.

Empathy can be a lot of things and can mean a lot of different things to different people. I feel that empathy can be described with these characteristics:

- Good listening skills
- Understanding what others are feeling
- Able to effectively build and manage others
- Show compassion and concern
- Relate to different perspectives or experience levels
- Able to relate to different age groups, seeing qualities in every generation
- Increased awareness and perspective of how things affect others
- Willing to give time and energy to others
- Support team members to own their power
- Demonstrate support and understanding to all cultures
- Possess good communication skills.

These are just a few characteristics—there are definitely more. But the important thing here is that we recognize what empathy is all about and how we can strengthen it within our self.

Today's leaders need to be more people focused. This can be tougher now, as we have technology that allows you to work in one state or one country, while your immediate boss works in another state or country, or even just another building. We have the highest levels ever, working from home and usually in their pajamas or comfy clothes, not in their professional attire or even ready for the day. We may not even see the person that oversees our position very often, if even at all. There is a vast need for these skills due to the lack of connection we are having as a society. Yes, technology is taking us places and is phenomenal. But we do have connection issues, and management gets to play a big part in making this part work. We have people that are unbelievably bright and intelligent, yet lack any serious common sense.

There have been studies out there done on major corporations, to see the need and the importance found in empathy. These studies were done to show how successful people are in their job performance, and how empathy was in relation to their job or position. This study was done across multi-cultural areas, and included over 35 countries. Across the board, they wanted to know answers to areas like this:

1. Are you willing to help an employee with personal problems?
2. Do you show interest in your team's hopes, their personal needs, or in their dreams?
3. Are you sensitive to signs of overwork in others?
4. Do you convey compassion towards them, when others disclose a personal loss?

They were also evaluated, by a superior or boss, who also rated them on three items that measured job performance. Here are the three additional areas:

- How would you rate this person's performance in their current position?
- Where would you place this person as a leader compared to the other leaders in your organization?
- What is the likelihood that this person will plateau, be demoted, or fired in the next five years based on their actions and behaviors as a manager?

If you do not think that this is a skill that you get to embrace, think again. If you are not measuring up to this criteria, you will not be easily employable, or stand out as a viable candidate, in the management and leadership world. Empathy has truly been tied to performance, and the simple practice of empathy was found to play a significant role.

"The Universe provides abundantly when you're in a state of Gratefulness." ~Wayne Dyer

I bring all of this up for you to actually see the importance and the value of both characteristics, and the role they play in our workforce. You do not have to chase this to be able to implement it. You get to recognize it for what it is and how it could best serve you. Allow the Universe to provide abundantly for you! You get to be aware of what is out there, and how you could be more connected, how you could take better action, and how you could up level your skill-set and your life, by being better with your empathy and your gratitude.

The other significant role we are seeing with leaders that lead with empathy, is the feeling of community in the workplace. Sure, gratitude is definitely a big part too, but people want to feel like they are understood, and appreciated. And the big one is that people need to belong!

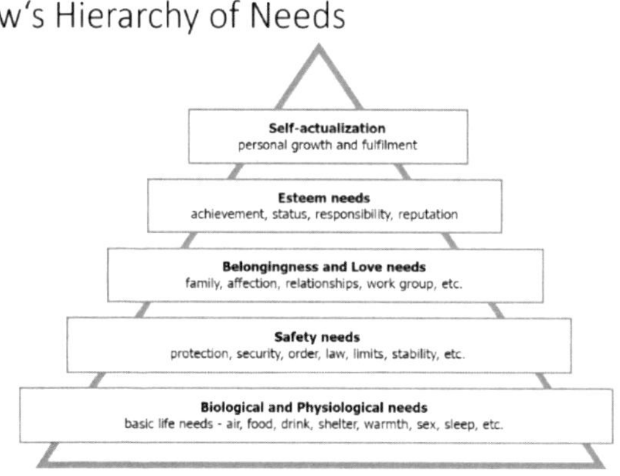

In Maslow's Hierarchy of Needs, belonging is one of our basic needs. It is crucial that we feel like we belong and are part of something bigger than ourselves. There has been study after study to agree with this and to support how important it is for us to feel like we belong.

We all want to belong to something bigger. We have a natural need for connection, and we thrive when we are supported and understood. Makes total sense that having a community feeling at our workplace would make us more committed to the success of the company as a whole. We are more willing to give it extra effort to hit a deadline, or push a little harder to put out a new product. Having community will create employee retention, employee engagement, and will raise the morale as a whole.

Embrace this if you are not already. Up-level where you are at, if you already do embrace it. We can all do better. We can all do more and can all BE more.

I love this song, probably because I could relate to the words and to some of where it goes. But more importantly, because it shows Genuine Gratitude. Being grateful for our challenges, for the lessons that we are learning, and for the scars that we have earned, gives us value and allows us to be whole and learn the bigger lesson. I would love to share the words with you:

Grateful By Rita Ora:

There were a lot of tears I had to cry through
A lot of battles left me battered and bruised
And I was shattered, had my heart ripped in two
I was broken, I was broken
There were a lot of times I stumbled and crashed
When I was on the edge, down to my last chance

So many times when I was so convinced that
I was over, I was over
But I had to fall yeah
To rise above it all

I'm grateful for the storm
Made me appreciate the sun
I'm grateful for the wrong ones
Made me appreciate the right ones
I'm grateful for the pain
For everything that made me break
I'm thankful for all my scars
'Cause they only make my heart
Grateful, grateful, grateful, grateful, grateful
Grateful

I was sinking, I was drowning in doubt
The weight, all of the pain, was weighing me down
Pulled it together and I pulled myself out
Learned a lesson, learned a lesson
That there's a lot you gotta go through, hell yes
But that's what got me strong, I got no regrets
And I've got only love, got no bitterness
Count my blessings, count my blessings, yeah
I'm proud of every tear, yeah
'Cause they got me here

I'm grateful for the storm
Made me appreciate the sun
I'm grateful for the wrong ones
Made me appreciate the right ones
I'm grateful for the pain
For everything that made me break
I'm thankful for all my scars
'Cause they only make my heart
Grateful, grateful, grateful, grateful, grateful
Grateful

There is nothing I would change
That even one mistake I made
I got lost, found myself, found my way

I'm grateful for the storm
Made me appreciate the sun
I'm grateful for the wrong ones
Made me appreciate the right ones
I'm grateful for the pain
For everything that made me break
I'm thankful for all my scars
'Cause they only make my heart
Grateful, grateful, grateful, grateful, grateful, oh
Grateful

You know that I'm grateful
You know that I care
No time for the wrong ones
I'll always be there
Grateful
Woah (Grateful, grateful, grateful)
I'm grateful, oh yeah (Grateful, grateful)
Oh, I'm grateful, yeah

Songwriter: Diane Eve Warren

May you find value in your struggles and challenges. And may you be grateful for what you have learned and what you will learn in the future. May you know within yourself how this will improve your life, and how you can move yourself forward in a huge way.

"Empathy and Gratitude allow us to go Beyond just Being Compassionate and Thankful. They allow us to build Trust, Honor and Respect." ~Kris Barney

TRAIT THREE:

CREATE Courageous Confidence

Cowardly Confidence vs Courageous Confidence

"Courageous Confidence is something you create within yourself by believing in who you are and who you are meant to be!"

"Change Your Inner Dialog and Watch how Fast Your Confidence Grows."

"We Create Our Own Reality when we Recognize what we are Doing and make the Corrections needed, we are Happier, Healthier and more Confident."

"Happiness comes from valuing, appreciating and acknowledging what we have, rather than focusing on what is missing."

Chapter 7

Cowardly Confidence vs Courageous Confidence

"Vulnerability is our most accurate measurement of Courage."
~Brene Brown

As human beings, we are creators. We begin the creation, or manifestation process, by first forming a thought or thought pattern in our mind. Our thoughts show up in the words we speak. Our actions are simply a manifestation of our thoughts and words. When our thoughts and actions come together, we get our results. My question for you is this—what results are you achieving, and are you satisfied with them, or would you like them to be different?"

Thoughts + Actions = Results

Have you ever stopped to think about just how much power our words have? It is amazing what power our words have. Our lives manifest what we tell ourselves.

Did you know that your own voice is your most believable voice? Yet we are harder on ourselves and say and think things about ourselves that we would never tolerate from someone else! How is that showing up for you? Are your own thoughts and words sabotaging you from being the best version of yourself?

Someone once said—Confidence is like a muscle, the more you use it the stronger it gets. Where is your level of confidence, and why do you feel the way you do? That is a question that is very important for us to ask ourselves so that we can evaluate how our life is going, where our confidence level is at, and what needs to change. Would it serve you to work your confidence muscle more regularly?

When we are confident we are happier. We are happier with our circumstances and we are happier with our relationships. As we own our confidence, we are stronger in our decisions, more dedicated to our goals, and more productive. So why wouldn't we want to be more confident?

When we do not own our confidence and build it to be courageous, we flounder it—and even go to great lengths to pretty much give it away. That may sound crazy, but think about it. Back in the dating scene, which for me was forever ago, but I have raised four children to grow to be adults that all dated before they got married. As we find a person we find attractive or we begin to like, it feels good. We get excited when they ask us out, and we are crushed if they don't. If they do ask us out and we build a relationship, as that relationship grows, we become more confident within our self and more at ease. We become more comfortable just being who we are, when we are around that person, because we are more confident in the relationship. We are more self-assured. We feel more self-worth. Yet if we do not build that relationship, we feel less than or not good enough. We feel like there is something wrong with us. We tend to be more withdrawn and don't even get me started about how awkward we become when that person is around. It really is true!

When we lack self-confidence, we feel vulnerable and can even feel fear of putting ourselves out there. Yet when we own our confidence, we are able to be very vulnerable and we share in a more authentic way, without feeling self-conscious or afraid of it. When we allow ourselves to embody confidence, and love who we are unconditionally, we are able to show up in a completely different way—in all different capacities of life. We are stronger as a parent, with a more solid connection with our spouse and our child. We are better in our significant relationships when we are confident with our self, rather than portraying a needy victim. We are more powerful in our work as we own our confidence and are assertive in creating a space where work is a beneficial part of our life. We become the person who is adding value wherever we go, rather than taking away value or being a complete taker. When we are confident, people are drawn to us and we become a very natural leader. We are influential and are able to make a real difference in the lives of those who are around us.

I teach that there are two types of Confidence: Cowardly Confidence and Courageous Confidence.

Cowardly Confidence comes from not believing in yourself, but rather looking to outward sources for your confidence. Confidence in yourself will never come from someone else. Your confidence must come from you. Someone else can give you great ideas or fantastic motivation, but you are the one who must maintain confidence, and that comes from believing in yourself and being willing to do the work to maintain that belief.

That means you must *decide* to be confident. Yes, making the DECISION is the first step. Then decide to love you. Decide to be all that you can be, and follow through with action! There are times when we come from a fear base of, "bad things happened to me and that is why I do not have confidence." There are circumstances in which this plays a part, but when we play the blame game, we are giving our power to others, and that is cowardly confidence. When we look to be validated by others, whether loved ones, co-workers, management, or peers, we are handing them our confidence card and then asking if we can have it back! This does not work! When we show up with confidence, others see that we own it. They feel assured with us. We come across more trustworthy and more intelligent.

Being overly confident, and playing it up in a cocky or arrogant way, is also a huge neon banner advertising someone who lacks confidence. This is someone who lacks self-confidence and is showing up in Cowardly Confidence. They are usually blaming everyone else if something goes wrong. They never take accountability and can often be caught not telling the whole truth. Their stories will be exaggerated, and you will be able to find holes in their stories. They can be found to have a hard time with authority, or have difficulty following another leader who actually has good confidence. This is showing up out of jealousy. And honestly, most people in this cycle do not even recognize it.

Now, let's talk about **Courageous Confidence**. Courageous Confidence is knowing that you are a powerful person and that you have gifts, talents, and abilities that are unique to you. It is loving yourself, even when you mess up and make a fool of yourself. It is knowing that you matter. It is knowing your value and holding yourself to those values. Being Courageously Confident takes daily work and constant redirection of thoughts that do not support what you are and who you are. It is about being who you want to be and accepting yourself in every part of that. It is knowing that you are enough and that you matter. It is about being all you can be and striving to continually progress and achieve higher levels. It is about knowing the only person you are in competition with is yourself, and you should only be trying to outdo you. The only comparison you should ever make is to how you could improve what happened in your yesterday to make your tomorrow even more amazing!

I teach an acronym for this: CREATE.

CREATE Courageous Confidence

C=Conquer: Conquer the voice inside your head. You get to believe in you. The most believable voice is your own. So embrace it, and have positive thoughts about yourself. Be willing to celebrate your accomplishments.

R=Reinforce: Reinforce by raising personal value and your character. Repeat 'I am' declarations, and create a list of accomplishments so you can see the proof as to why you are so amazing. Use a vision board to show where you want your life to go, and so you can see it every day. Then reinforce how your confidence in yourself will allow you to achieve your dreams.

E=Evaluate: Evaluate and examine where you are and what needs to change. Discover how you can improve each day. Evaluate your progress and your failures, so that you can know what are trigger points or setbacks. Evaluate when times are good and you are feeling more confident, and find what works the most and the best for you. Own it.

A=Accept: Accept where you are. Begin there. We all have 'reasons' as to where our confidence has either come from or been taken away by. It doesn't matter where you are—what matters is what you do about it, and that you do it differently. Does the value of a human being change? NO. We are all born with the exact same amount of value. And at the end of life, it remains the same. Human value does not depend on how much money you make or at what level you are in the workplace. Actual human value does not change.

T=Trust: Trust the process. Trust yourself. Your own words are the most powerful for you.

Expect greatness, trust that you deserve it, and trust when it happens. Stop doubting yourself. See yourself the way you want others to see you, and trust that they will and that they do see you.

"Courageous Confidence is something you create within yourself by believing in who you are and who you are meant to be!" ~Kris Barney

Chapter 8

Who Are You Listening to Anyway—Believe in You

"You must learn a new way to think before you can master a new way to be." ~Marianne Williamson

One of the biggest culprits to our losing confidence is our self-talk. I am talking specifically about our thoughts—the words we actually say, and the inner dialogue or chatter that is constantly going on inside our heads and coming out of our mouths. We need to be very conscious of our thoughts and words. Each thought we have is the first step to creating or manifesting something. Our subconscious wants to be right, and is willing to do what it takes. Where do you think those thoughts really come from? Who are you listening to anyway?

What does your inner dialogue sound like? What would your friends hear if your thoughts were broadcast out loud? Would they hear things like, "No matter what I do, I can't win. There just never seems to be enough money to go around. Nobody really wants to hear what I have to say. Nobody likes my ideas, anyway. I'll never find a good job. I'm ugly and fat. I'm an ugly duckling, right?" I want you to really think about this. What are you saying to yourself when no one else is listening?

Have you ever watched ducks on a pond? They just seem to float around effortlessly, dipping their beaks into the water to snatch some yummy little tidbit of food. Even though their movements seem effortless, we know that underneath the surface of the water there is actually a whole lot of activity going on.

You see, ducks have a secret weapon—webbed feet! A duck controls its maneuverings on the surface of the pond by the movement of its legs underneath the surface. It can go anywhere it wants simply by changing the speed and intensity of either one, or both legs. The intensity and speed become significant if there is danger, if there is competition for food, or if they are playing and they want to win.

Without realizing it, we are much the same way. Have you ever noticed that some people seem to live a charmed life—yet for others, nothing seems to go right? Like a duck on a pond, many of our results and the places we end up, are a direct result of what is going on underneath the surface. It is the speed and intensity by which we do things that propels us to where we are today. But instead of having webbed feet, we have our Self-Talk and our Positive Thoughts—these are our secret weapons—and they determine our speed, intensity, and direction. If we learn to monitor and manage our Self-Talk, the way that a duck does its webbed feet, our lives will go much smoother, with more yummy tidbits tossed our way.

Once a person's inner dialogue and goals are in harmony, life gets easier and they accomplish more. Abundance begins to flow, self-esteem raises, and life feels so much better.

"Change Your Inner Dialogue and Watch how Fast Your Confidence Grows." ~Kris Barney

Your secret weapon is Self-Talk! Positive self-talk will literally change your whole world! Your inner dialogue and thoughts must become a determined focus for you. You must be willing to pay attention and make the changes needed to have the results you want. Make sure that what's going on under the surface is propelling you in the direction that you actually want to go.

Here are some things you can do to improve your self-talk, as well as gain more confidence and find the courage to believe in yourself.

- **Love Yourself:** This can be a tough one. Yet if we do not love and respect ourselves, who will? Love yourself where you are—because things won't change until you do. As you love yourself, you will be able to love others more. Be careful not to judge yourself or your journey. We are all on a journey—and if we stop the judgment and embrace the journey, we will improve our courageous confidence!

- **Stop Criticism**: Especially to yourself! Never allow bad questions or self-defeating questions into your mind. And never speak or think questions like: "Why am I so stupid? Why am I so fat? Why do I always break things? Why am I such a failure?" It is amazing that we think and say negative things about and to ourselves, that we would never say about one of our friends, or even our enemies. Be conscious of the thoughts you allow to "hang out" in your mind. Our subconscious wants to be right. So if you are thinking and saying things that are not good things, your own subconscious will try to make it right. No Negatives.

- **Stop Frightening Thoughts:** I have heard it said that frightening thoughts are just negative affirmations. Watch yourself when you feel frightening thoughts. They will go to the subconscious. When you feel this happening, go to a happy thought—like walking on the beach or watching a sunset. Create a happy thought pattern that you can go to when you feel fear, or have frightening thoughts.

- **Ask Only Good Questions:** One way to focus on the positive is to ask yourself good questions like: "Why am I so amazing? Why am I so inspirational?" Positive declarations are helpful. These can be easy. Write little positive phrases on small pieces of paper, and put them in places where you see them often—like your mirror or the refrigerator. Read them and repeat them to yourself. This can be used for anything you want to work on. I have found them to be powerful in creating positive changes. You can have notes on your phone, reminders in your car, and positive thoughts on your computer. Have them at work, at home, and make them available for you to see wherever you spend the most time each day.

Self-Talk can be a tough one. It took me quite a while to be positive with myself! I strive constantly to keep it in check. We all do. This is something that takes constant reinforcement and will require consistent work all along the way. It is not just a designation we earn, and then forever tout it to be true. We can get knocked down easily, and sometimes it can even blind side us when we least expect it.

Story: Crucial Conversations

Not that long ago, I submitted for the opportunity to keynote on a huge stage. I went through several interviews with the presidents of three separate associations that were coming together for this yearly conference. From what I had been told, I stood a great possibility of landing this job. This would put me in front of thousands of people who could then hire me as a speaker, and would have a huge impact on my career.

I sat on pins and needles. I was ecstatic to even be considered. I felt a ton of confidence even after the interviews. Two of the presidents had said something like, “I think you are a perfect fit for our conference.”

The board that would be deciding on the final keynote spot, met together and discussed all of the options they had, and those they felt strongest about. A decision was made.

Have you ever been so excited for something that is about to happen for you—something that could change life as you now know it? How did that feel? Were you excited? Yep, me too! Did you lose sleep? Yep, me too! I was like a kid in the candy store with a wad full of cash and options galore.

I got the phone call. It was one of the presidents that I had interviewed with. He said, “I am really sorry, but we have chosen to go a different direction.”

WHAT??? They needed a female speaker. They wanted it to be leadership with a new perspective. They didn’t even have to fly me in, because I lived within driving distance. And they had loved me. WHY?

I mustered up all the courage I could find at that moment and asked, “Do you mind telling me who you decided on?" He said, "Crucial Conversations." But I would like to bring you in on another occasion.

I was devastated. My life as I knew it felt over. I had worked so hard. I immediately got into my head with the negative chatter. My confidence, and even courage, went out the window. I moved everything off my calendar for the rest of the afternoon and decided to have my own little pity party. I began convincing myself that I wasn't worth it. I had no value as a speaker, and why was I even doing this anyway. It was just too hard!

Let me set this stage a bit for you. I am a one girl show—Me, Myself, and I—when it comes to speaking. Yes, my husband and I have our corporation together and we do really well. But in reality, I am small potatoes in the great big world of speakers. I am a leadership and communication speaker—the most popular and flooded class of speakers out there. Literally thousands and thousands of speakers fit in this area. Yet, after getting more of the conversation, and finding out a bit of what took place, I found out that one of the decision makers had an "IN" with Crucial Conversations. They came in for FREE and spoke at this conference. THEY ARE A MULTI-MILLION DOLLAR CORPORATION! Yet, I am bleeding on the floor upset, and convincing myself that I am not good enough. SERIOUSLY, we are not even in the same league! Why would I EVER allow this to upset me like it did? Why would I not embrace that little old me went up against a major hitter—and I did not do so bad. Right?

Have you found yourself in a similar situation? Have you given your all to get that promotion at work, and they chose someone that does not have the experience or even the education that you have? Perhaps you asked your crush out for a date, and you got turned down. Maybe you had hopes and dreams for your children, and they chose their own path that doesn't quite look like you thought it would.

Do you find yourself saying things like, "I can't do this!" or "I am so stupid!"? Do you find yourself questioning who you are or doubting your abilities? When we doubt ourselves, our subconscious wants to be right. It will go to great lengths to prove to us that we are right. So, be careful with this. Catch yourself and correct it immediately. Tell yourself that you can do it and that you will do it. Reinforce the positive whenever you feel doubt or fear at all. Empower yourself. It will support you in your positive thought processes. It may seem silly, but consider this: if you were to say the things that run through your mind to your spouse, or even your child, how would they feel? That is what you are doing to yourself when you allow negative self-talk. So STOP IT!

When you get off track, choose to realign, and do it immediately. You have freedom to choose how you respond to life, so choose positivity. Know WHO you are and BE IT! If you feel like you are not sure of who you are, write down what that would be for you. What do you want it to look like? How would it feel to own that? Remind yourself of that several times a day.

Watch how fast your life begins to change, and starts to look like what you are telling yourself you are. Things like, "I am releasing weight and feeling great, and I gratefully acknowledge and accept it now." It is amazing!

Go ahead—write yourself a positive declaration—and repeat it multiple times a day. Say it as if it has already taken place and watch how your life aligns to it. It is powerful. I suggest to my clients to use these simple ways to begin their declarations. Start with positive statements in the first person. Speak them as if they have already happened, and see yourself in an accomplishment mentality to accomplish your goals. I start each statement with one of the following phrases, or one like it:

- I am
- I create
- I release
- I inspire
- I love
- I trust
- I know
- I believe
- I live
- I empower
- I attract

Make sure you are saying your declarations three times a day: first thing in the morning, once during the day, and last thing before you go to bed so that your subconscious mind works on them all night.

You have got this. You can do it. You are worth it! I Believe in You—and YOU should TOO!

"We Create Our Own Reality when we Recognize what we are Doing and Make the Corrections needed, we are Happier, Healthier and more Confident." ~Kris Barney

Chapter 9

Happiness is a Choice

"When one door of happiness closes, another opens; but often we look so long at the closed door that we do not see the one which has been opened for us." Helen Keller

We can choose to be happy, even when our circumstances are not the best and we may even be struggling. Happiness is seriously a choice. Self-confidence soars when we are happy. We believe in ourselves, and become less self-conscious and awkward. We laugh and enjoy other people around us—and life just plain goes better. You first need to be willing to be flexible and adapt to your situations easily. This means even when things are not going well, you can still be happy and enjoy the moments in your life.

Story: The Santa Suit

I learned this lesson many years ago. I had been married for two and a half years. We had one child, and we were thrilled to be new parents. Parenthood is a happy time for everyone, Right? Well, at the time we were doing everything that we could to provide for ourselves and raise our baby boy. I was a 'stay at home mommy' at that point in our life, and my husband worked as a mechanic in an auto shop. We had a very happy life together, despite many difficulties. I am not going to go into a lot of the challenges—but rather, this story is one in which we really got to just choose to be happy.

The delivery of my son required surgery. And in the end, our insurance did not pay very well on our medical bills. This became quite a burden on us financially, in addition to the new expenses of adding another person in our life—we all know how much a baby can really cost. Before we knew it, we really did need to have more income. I had an executive secretarial degree from college, and decided to go back to work—with limited hours so that I could also spend time with my son. I found a startup business that I could work for that would allow me to take my son with me. The catch was that they were going to pay me in a lump sum when the funding from the investors came through. I decided this was perfect for us. I would be able to take my baby with me, and we would have the money in time for Christmas.

As the weeks went on and I had to work many hours without pay, I finally called it quits. After all, this was not making our situation better—it was making it worse. We took them to small claims court. They indeed owed me money and were legally obligated to pay me, if and when they could. It was so unexpected that we were really not prepared for what was happening. As that year came into the holiday season, we could see that we would barely make enough money to cover the necessary bills, if that, and that we would NOT be having Christmas.

We were actually fine with that, for the most part. After all, we had each other and were doing ok. We chose not to tell anyone about it. We would be happy & cheerful, and nobody needed to know. We agreed to not get gifts for each other. We also made the decision to sell my husband's saddle, which he loved, and my stereo, which I loved, to come up with enough money to buy gifts for our extended families and the gift exchanges. That way, no one would know that we were struggling financially and it would all be ok. This was absolutely amazing! We just chose to be happy, even though our circumstances were bleak. I had not remembered another time when I had to just choose to be happy, and believe wholeheartedly it would all be ok.

I began to do odd things here and there to earn little bits of money to help out—like tend the neighbor’s children, and sell some crafts that I made. As I did this, I was able to take a few dollars here and there to put together to save.

The December before this, we had been able to drive a friend around as Santa Claus. I was eight months pregnant with our first child then. I remember how much fun we had as we watched “Santa” surprise people, bringing happiness & joy to them as he barged into their houses. We were the ‘getaway car’! It was so much fun that my husband had been wanting a Santa suit all year. All he wanted for Christmas was to make others happy, and to spread joy to everyone—and a Santa suit could do that.

Well, I went to work. I began secretly sewing his costume and gathering the items needed, such as leather boots, a belt, bells, a very expensive beard, and so on. He had no idea. It was so exciting, and it totally took my focus off of our destitute situation. I got it all together, finished sewing the final touches, and wrapped up this huge box in fabulous Santa wrapping paper.

We had a special birthday party, for his mother’s birthday, on December 12th. He came home from work and I told him that I had a surprise for him, but there was one stipulation. He had to wear it to the birthday party with his whole family. I had sewn several things before this. So when he started at me with, "We agreed to not buy any gifts for each other this year...," I told him that I had just sewed him something. So he probably thought it was a western shirt or something that was not a big deal.

When he opened his gift, all he could do was cry. I have never seen him so happy. He wore the costume to the party, and even his mother sat on his lap and did not know who he was. I remember her saying, "That Santa sure did know a lot of details about all of the family!"

That was the beginning of one of our best Christmases ever! We took every dime that we could come up with and bought candy canes and gas to put in the car. Every night, we went door to door surprising everyone with Santa barging in and bringing happiness & joy to everyone. No one had any idea that we were not having Christmas at our house. After all, our son was not even a year old. He only needed a couple of little toys, diapers and formula. We chose to be happy and to spread happiness everywhere. To this day, we have people talk to us and tell us how they remember, over 30 years ago, when we stopped by and made their whole Christmas!

I discovered that being happy is a choice. By choosing to be happy, it truly blesses our lives. Yes, there were times when I had to dig deep to find that happiness—but the rewards were well worth it. Nobody wants to be around someone who is not happy. I mean, really? Who wants that?

It is so much more fun to be around the person who is the life of the party, or the friendliest one to be with. Chances are, the happiest person in the room is the happiest, because they choose to be. If you were to know what was really going on in their world, they probably do not have it the easiest, or the best job, or the most money, or the nicest house, or the most handsome husband. They are just choosing to make the best of life and to be happy in every situation. They will be healthier and happier, and will live longer than the stressed out, miserable, whiny person.

Story: The Party

It has been proven that our emotions will cause dis-ease, and it is true! I have lived this. I have had fibromyalgia and neuropathy for many years now. I am pretty sure that they were both originally brought on by stress, depression, and buried emotions. When I choose to be happy and flexible in my life, my fibromyalgia & neuropathy are very manageable. I can pretty much deal with them both through natural remedies, healthy eating, exercise, and essential oils. But when I allow the stress to take over in my life, or I do not choose to be happy about the trials I am going through, or I allow contention into my life, I will have a huge flare up in my fibromyalgia and neuropathy. It works just like clockwork. If I allow myself to get upset, I will *feel* it for days. Once I learned how I could literally make a decision to choose to be happy anyway, and it would make a huge difference in how I felt, that made the choice much easier! Yes, it takes practice and a conscious effort on my part. But when I choose to have my life work for me by being happy, I feel so much better.

One night many years ago, my husband and I attended a party. We were happy to go. We had not seen most of the people there for quite a while, and we love these people. We were on our way there, but were driving through a storm. Now when there is a storm, my fibromyalgia goes into overdrive and flares up like crazy. I was in a lot of pain and very uncomfortable. But I did not want this to inhibit how my night at this get-together would be. I pushed the discomfort and pain aside and focused on being happy. I focused on being able to attend a party, having these amazing people in my life, and how great it was to be out and enjoying life.

As the evening went on, I was having a great time. I was visiting with everyone, and enjoying myself despite the situation. I never uttered a word about the pain or discomfort—just focused on the happiness.

At this party, there was another woman who also had fibromyalgia. She had a significant case, with similar issues as what I have. The entire night she complained about her pain. She wanted to be doted on, and was very negative. Everyone began to avoid her, and pretty soon she was alone. She had been negative about everything—from the food, to gossiping about the people in attendance and those who were not even there. Everyone was sick of her. Nobody really even wanted to listen to her at that point. She ended up getting her husband to leave the party early and went home. In fact, they did not even stay for much over an hour. But the entire room felt the energy shift the minute she left. Everyone felt relief to have her gone.

How sad is that? I know her well and love her very much. Yet I could not deny the relief that came when the negative was removed. When we are consumed with negative, we do not even recognize how we are coming off. She felt like it was a horrible party and talked about just how rotten it was for a long time after. Yet everyone else stayed for hours, laughing and having a great time.

It is interesting what our perspective is on things when we are happy, verses when we are angry or in pain or frustrated. When we can keep things in check, and we strive to show up with confidence and happiness, our lives are so much better.

This same thing happens at work. Think about a meeting where the boss was upset, or a manager was ticked off. How did the meeting go? It is truth, I promise you. The happier you are, the more confidence you have in making your decisions and in following through on your commitments. It just works.

All of us have heard miraculous stories of someone on their deathbed, who has decided that they do not want to die. What happens? They become cured of an incurable disease. This does happen. My own father-in-law was proof of this. He had deteriorating health for years. He had been on his deathbed several times. In fact, on one particular occasion, he had been rushed to the hospital. He was so bad, and his heart was failing to the point that they called all of the children and we rushed down to say our goodbyes. He was so bad that they did not even put him into the hospital as an inpatient, but rather had us in a back room of the emergency department. Guess what happened? He had the realization that he might really die—and POOF. He lived for another five full years, on his own and in his own house!

Happiness is literally a choice. So, why would you not choose happiness? If you want to be happy, then choose to be happy. I know this is easier said than done. But, just think about this—we have all had a friend or family member that we have spent time with. This person is always complaining, and everything bad that could possibly happen has and will happen to them. I bet you can think of that person right now. Do you want to spend more time with them, or do you try to avoid having to go with them or be around them? We avoid those types of people. You know you have done this! You have avoided them because they are negative.

What type of people do you choose to surround yourself with? Are they happy, friendly people, or are they stressed out, miserable, whiney people? Being happy is a choice—so I suggest that you make your choices count. By choosing to be happy, you will experience more opportunities to have happiness in your life.

Happiness is a huge factor in our self-confidence, and with our self-worth. When you have more happiness, you have more confidence. When you choose to find the good in your challenges, you have more courage, strength, and confidence to go through your challenges. When you are willing to be happy, despite your circumstances, things will go better in your life—Guaranteed!

"Happiness comes from valuing, appreciating, and acknowledging what we have—rather than focusing on what is missing." ~Kris Barney

TRAIT FOUR:

EXCEL in Exceptional Excellence

Enough Excellence vs Exceptional Excellence

"Change Your Inner Dialogue and Watch how Fast Your Confidence Grows."

"Exceptional Excellence is living your full potential while inspiring others to do the same."

"Everyone has the power within them to conquer any challenge life throws at them and be stronger because of it!"

Chapter 10

Enough Excellence vs Extraordinary Excellence

"We are what we repeatedly do; therefore Excellence is not an act but a habit." ~Aristotle

When you focus on problems, you will have more problems. When you focus on possibilities, you will have more opportunities! When you focus on being the best you can be, you excel to Exceptional Excellence! Living in Exceptional Excellence allows us to have Exceptional Lives! Start by striving to be all that you can be—willing to continually push out of your comfort zone, wanting more and better.

Exceptional Excellence takes courage and strength, as well as always keeping your word. It takes responsible leadership, and will fail without honesty and integrity. Sound tough? Yes, it is. That is why there are so few people who live in Exceptional Excellence consistently. But that does not mean that it isn't worth it! Those who 'do' are high achievers—the ones who live the life of their dreams!

Marianne Williamson said, "You must learn a new way to think before you can master a new way to be."

She's right. We must first learn a new way to think. Decisions and choices come originally from our thoughts! The things we decide in our heads become our reality. Exceptional Excellence has to be a focus and a desire from within. We must commit to stay the course to accomplish it! It is not easy to be committed to extraordinary excellence, but the payoff is so worth it. When we see people at this level of excellence, we see them as being influential, inspiring, productive, successful, and many other admirable traits. It even looks as if it may be easy when watching them. But what you do not see is all the time they have spent to improve themselves enough to be to this point. It is attainable for us all, but it will not be easy.

The other thing that becomes our reality is what we seek. I share many stories and things I do, and things we do as a family, to seek for good. It becomes a way of life. Pretty soon you do not even realize you are searching for good—it becomes second nature—and things show-up for you, if you are purposefully living that way. Ideas and opportunities to do good just fall in your lap, when this becomes a focus for you.

For over 20 years, our family has been sponsoring girls in Ethiopia. We pay for their schooling, their school clothes, and their supplies. We have never met the girls we sponsor, but we have had their pictures on our refrigerator, and usually a card that they send us each year. I do not tell you this to brag. I tell you this because there are ways to do this easily. There are charitable programs out there everywhere! Seek out the one that touches your heart, and allow yourself to get involved in whatever way works for you. For us, this came from changing our focus and being open to striving for exceptional excellence. It came because we wanted to up-level our lives.

My questions for you are these: What could you be doing at a higher level? What is your level of excellence today? What are you seeking? I promise, you are receiving what you are seeking. As hard and frank as that is—it is truth. What you seek, you find—at every level of your life.

Let's break this down a bit. I believe there are two views of Excellence: **Enough Excellence and Exceptional Excellence**.

Enough Excellence is just that—you are enough. You do well for yourself. You are a good person. You are above average and you give back. Here are some things for you to consider as I describe some attributes of Enough Excellence:

- You go about your day doing what you need to do, and living up to your agreements.
- You keep your commitments and do your responsibilities pretty well.
- You have good relationships.
- You do a good job and are successful.
- You have accomplished much and you are content.
- You keep your word, for the most part, and you are dependable.
- Your integrity is good, and you are a good spouse or partner, and parent.
- You know that your health is a priority and that you should probably focus more on it.
- You are fairly giving, and serve others.
- Your confidence is good, and you do a pretty good job in fulfilling your duties.
- You are above average, and would be considered somewhat middle class. If grades were to be given in life, you would rank right up there in that B range, even perhaps a B+. Although rare, you have seen some areas where you did slip down into the C range.

Now let's go over attributes of what it would look like to be in Exceptional Excellence. Exceptional Excellence is going above expectation. It is about having no limitation. It is being the very best you can be and continually working for improvement. It is about having vision and direction, as well as taking action and follow through. Let me give you a list to consider about Exceptional Excellence:

- You are amazing. You are always on your A game and are never ok with average.
- You go the extra mile in all aspects of your life.
- Your relationships are flourishing. People love to be around you. You are an example to everyone.
- You put others first always, and your leadership and confidence show it.
- Your success is off the charts! You are punctual. You are prepared, and you are obedient.
- There is no limitation for you except the sky!
- You have impeccable integrity. You keep your word.
- You pay off obligations early, and keep all your commitments.
- You are organized. You are a leader and change lives.
- Your health is in the forefront. You eat well nutritionally, and exercise your body regularly.
- You are a phenomenal spouse or partner, and a committed, loving parent.
- You are successful in business and finances, and it shows up in all that you do.
- You see accomplishments on a daily basis, and you cannot wait to achieve the next goal.

- You have vision and direction in all that you do, and continually dream of what you can accomplish to up-level your life.
- You serve others continually, and are always outward focused. You are creative, innovative, and open to the next step for you and your success.
- You are confident, dependable, charismatic, honest, humble, passionate, caring, successful, loving, and happy.
- You love your life and all that is in it!

Perhaps that list sounds like a ton of work, maybe stressful, and even unattainable. What I want you to know is that as we seek and work for these things, they become automatic. When we are willing to work hard at being an exceptional person, this list becomes the by-product. When we put phenomenal plans in place, and create a system to get there, we can achieve anything that we want! Anyone can achieve this. It is attainable. What you also get to know is that we are always a work in progress. We may be great in thirteen areas on the above list, but need to focus our efforts in four of the areas. What you get to know is that as you align yourself with a genuine desire to perform your life with exceptional excellence, things really do align. As you get more organized and improve your health, you will find you get a promotion, which comes with higher pay and now allows you to give to charity, pay off your house, and be of service more often. Does this make sense? It all comes together as you work towards the goal.

I have an acronym for this:

EXCEL in Exceptional Excellence

E=Execute and Engage: Must be able to execute, take huge action, and engage what you want. Execute on your goals and high performance. Engage with your team and your leaders to create excellence in the workplace. Engage others to also be in exceptional excellence.

X=X-ray: Look deeper inside. Look for hairline fractures in all aspects of your work and performance. Get a mentor, manager, or a colleague to give you a second opinion on goals, action steps, and performance.

C=Choice: This is a choice. Choose what you want. Be willing to do the work. Make the decision and keep going even when it is tough. Make the choice to be exceptional no matter what. Be aware of who you are choosing to spend time with. Make the choice for personal improvement.

E=Efficiency: Create a plan to be effective. Have efficiency on your side. Create systems and ways to raise the bar for you and for your teams, and be more effective. Be diligent and consistent to create the momentum to have the levels of efficiency you want.

L=Loyal: Be loyal to yourself. Be loyal to your plan. Be loyal to commitments. Be loyal to your values. Be loyal to exceptional excellence. Create your team to be loyal. Be loyal to your team. Be loyal to your company. Create a loyal community.

Be willing to be flexible, and adapt to your situations easily. We can choose to be in our excellence even when our circumstances are less than great, and when we may even be struggling. Excellence is a choice.

Yes, it takes practice and conscious effort on your part. But when you choose to have your life work for you, you will feel so much better. The biggest thing for you to remember is that you have a choice! You are the one choosing your decisions and creating the life you are leading. Why not choose Excellence?

I suggest that you bloom where you are planted. This means—Be the best YOU always—wherever you may be in life. It means to start where you are. If you are in Enough Excellence, and you are ready to up-level to Exceptional Excellence, take note of what needs to change to get you into that next step for you. It is much easier to be happy with where you are in life, than to constantly be upset about it. If you are not quite at Enough Excellence, find a goal that can get you to the next level.

Ask yourself these questions: What do I want my life to be like? How can I have more joy in my life? What would it take to raise my excellence? Where do I want to start? Then create your plan and implement execution of that plan. I suggest and teach creating a 90 day goal. After you have decided and visualized what you want it to look like in 90 days, go back through and determine what level you must achieve at 60 days. Then do it again to set the pace at 30 days, and determine what the 30 day goal is. Once you have broken it down in this way, you now have your plan for the next four weeks. If you will do this in all areas that you want to work on, it can become a very powerful program for you to move yourself to the next level. It does not have to be hard or complicated—but it does have to be consistent and focused. Your success begins and ends with you. Isn't it up to you to take the action necessary to get where you want to be?

I have heard it said that the 'going the extra mile lane' is never crowded. When we are in our exceptional excellence, we are in that going the extra mile lane. In this lane, there is no speed limit. You are allowed to go at the fastest rate possible. You can arrive to your next destination ahead of schedule if you so choose. There will be obstacles, but nothing you can't handle. It will be exhilarating to feel the breeze blowing through your hair as you forge forward in your convertible race car. Only the best of the best get to go in this lane, and you have earned it.

Excellence is literally a choice. So why would you not choose Exceptional Excellence? If you want excellence, choose excellence. Make your choice count. By choosing to be in your excellence, you will experience more opportunities to have excellence in your life

Life is not so much about what happens to you as it is about how you choose to feel about it, and what you do with it.

"Everyone has the power within them to conquer any challenge life throws at them and be stronger because of it!" ~ Kris Barney

Chapter 11

Exceptional Excellence in the Workplace

"Treat a man as he is and he will remain as he is. Treat a man as he can and should be, and he will become as he can and should be." ~Stephen R. Covey

Our world has diversity like never before. As a leader, we get to lead our teams with qualities like exceptional excellence, where we can show empathy and understanding to diverse beliefs, emotions, or orientations—while still managing and directing a project or a team with cooperation and commitment to the team and company.

We will have all different issues that will arise. And we must be willing to dig deep inside for the skills and abilities to create unity and strength, as well as build connection and community together. I like what Stephen Covey said: "Treat a man as he is and he will remain as he is. Treat a man as he can and should be, and he will become as he can and should be." As leaders, we must treat others as they can and should be, to raise them up and build trust, honor, and respect. In our business world today, as a leader, we must have the qualities it takes to create effective teams that are productive, profitable, and successful. It will require that you put all 7 Traits that I teach, into effect in a real way—and continually focus on how to up-level yourself first, as you lead and empower others. Excellent leadership is inspiring and empowering when done effectively.

We talked about Empathy in the section on Gratitude. Empathy has become huge in our workplace, as we have such diversity in our colleges and in our businesses. Embrace Empathy with your struggling colleagues, and support them. So that as a team and business, you meet your deadlines, you finish your projects, and your work gets done well. Think about it—when we step up and assist someone going through a tough time, it builds trust and connection. If we throw them under the bus when they are struggling already, they will just become the weak link in the chain—and as we know, that one weak link can weaken the entire chain. We have all heard it before—you are only as strong as your weakest link.

If you are the leader over the entire group, you will be seen differently if you are not supportive and understanding. It will build a wedge into how much respect they have for you, and how much you deserve, and the entire group may lose trust in you. If you are a leader over a specific group or project, when you show up with empathy and understanding, this will allow for your supervisor or manager—even your boss—to see you as a leader. You will be magnifying those skills that they desire in those that they promote into higher responsibility positions. It only works in your favor—and it is the right thing to do. We will all face different times of challenge, and we all have times when we deserve the support and cooperation of a community and team we can count on. As the leader, it is also your responsibility to bring out the best in the people on your team—and how better to lead, than through example.

As business leaders, we know that in business—results matter. Results affect everything, especially our bottom line. And let's face it, if that does not exist, we go belly up. We want our teams to be driven, excited, and all in. We want their mindset to be focused and their ability to be off the charts. This happens when teams are led by inspiration and enthusiasm. These are qualities found in exceptional excellence. When we are living true to these principles, the qualities naturally appear. You have pride in your work and in yourself, which allows you to be enthusiastic in enrolling others with you.

As you lead with confidence and excellence, you are driven to perform and to get the positive results you desire. We have all been around that person who does not take no for an answer. That is a person driven and focused on a goal and an outcome that they desire. This is what you get to embrace as you lead and direct your team. The way you engage rubs off on everyone around you, and it raises everyone else's belief, confidence, and desire to move forward. Here is a list of things that I feel are pertinent qualities, traits, and values found in a leader:

- Show up in Sincere Service
- Grow in Genuine Gratitude
- Create Courageous Confidence
- Excel in Exceptional Excellence
- Live in Lasting Love
- Create Complete Communication
- Implement Impeccable Integrity

Yes, of course I feel that those are the answers, right? They are the 7 Traits that I teach. But as we live those traits fully, here are the effects that you will see in this leader:

- Always Prepared
- Passionate and Enthusiastic
- Results Oriented and Thinks Outside the Box
- Proactive and Well Planned
- Skilled, Talented, and is Continually Learning
- Solves Problems Easily and Manages Change Well
- Original and Confident
- Understands People and Embraces Empathy
- Serves and Assists Other Colleagues
- Always Striving to Up-Level
- Embraces Teamwork and is an Effective Team Player
- Resilient and Resourceful
- Produces Results while Promoting Others
- Cooperates with and Finds Value in Others
- Works in a Team and for the Team
- Welcomes Feedback and Assists Others to Rise
- Embraces the Highest Integrity
- Supportive, Builds Unity, Loyalty and Trust
- Acknowledges Others and Shows Appreciation
- Has Vision and Makes Decisions Easily

Of course that list is not all, but gives you a good idea of what it encompasses. When we live as an Exceptionally Excellent person, those are the results we see. Think of who you look up to in your arena. Are they living in this way? Why are they your hero?

"My mother said to me, 'If you become a soldier, you'll be a general. If you become a monk, you'll end up as the pope.' Instead, I became a painter, and wound up as Picasso." ~Pablo Picasso

We get to be OUR BEST SELF! As we do this as a leader, we build community in the workplace. It is built on loyalty, trust, and unity. As we build this, we must be willing to show acknowledgement to others for their part on our team. We get to recognize their accomplishments and build them up. We get to show our appreciation and gratitude, as well as be of service to them. When we do this, we build strong teams. We create a safe place for people to thrive. We build strength within our group, and the group becomes supportive of each other and recognizes the value of each and every person. They grow into a group that embodies lasting love, and they support each other despite their diversity or differing beliefs.

Courageous confidence comes in as we believe in ourselves, and in those leading our group. As we raise confidence across the entire group, it allows us to keep fear out. Fear of failure is something that holds us back. We can have fear as a complete business, as a team, or even as a leader. Fear can stop you or propel you…the choice is yours! Do not forget that we can turn fear into massive motivation, if properly channeled. But it can also stop us of all forward momentum, if we allow it to win. When we empower our entire team to feel valued, accepted, and worthy, they will surprise you at what can be accomplished. We must be willing to see new ideas or opportunities—while not fearing failure or lack of successful. Fear has the potential to limit you as a leader. Be aware of it, and on top of it.

All exceptionally excellent leaders are good at making decisions. Decision making is huge. To do this, you have to have vision. You must know where you are headed, and anticipate what is needed and must be put into place. As a leader you get to be good at change. Change is inevitable, and as a leader you must anticipate and prepare for those things constantly. You get to have effective training programs and practices that build the skills needed for leadership experiences. You get to lead them by challenging

them to move forward, inspiring them to live up to their responsibilities, and giving them opportunity to grow and live in their full potential. This is important, as it will allow them to build character and self-esteem. We should all be given an opportunity to grow and advance and be supported while getting there. No leader has ever made it to where they are without mentors, leaders and examples paving the way.

With all of this said, I am sure you see the importance of Exceptional Excellence in the workplace, and its significant role. But also keep in mind what this would mean to your relationships outside of work, with those you hold dearest to your heart. How would living this way change how you are showing up, and the quality of your life? We are the leader in our own life. We are getting the results from our leadership. Perhaps this is a good place to take a look at what you could change.

"Exceptional Excellence is living your full potential, while inspiring others to do the same." ~Kris Barney

Chapter 12

Oh That Brother of Mine

"No matter how many mistakes you make or how slow you progress, you're still way ahead of everyone who isn't trying."
~Tony Robbins

It was a bitter cold day, twenty years ago. My life as I knew it would never be the same. It was February 8, 1999 when I received that dreaded phone call. Yes, the one we never want to receive. My twin brother was dead.

Let me tell you a bit about my twin brother, Kirk. If ever there was someone who had the potential to live in their excellence, it was Kirk—although, he did not always embrace it. He was charismatic, funny, intelligent, coordinated, popular, athletic, brilliant, brave, dedicated, and a winner. He could do anything he set his mind to. He had all the talent you could imagine, and won awards right and left for anything and everything. He was a master craftsman and a general contractor, when he decided this world would be better off without him. That is when he took his own life.

Yes, twenty years ago I gave the hardest speech I have ever given in my life. I was a speaker at my twin brother's funeral. It seems so crazy that I am now a speaker by choice. For part of the tribute, my husband and I wrote a poem, and I want to share it with you.

OH THAT BROTHER OF MINE

'Twas the 25th of April that brought great joy.
A cute little girl and a bouncing boy.
With parents surprised to find it was twins,
"Honey," she screamed, "...go buy diapers and pins!"
Two cribs were needed to keep us apart.
But Kirk was determined, and so he would start,
To rock on his knees in that crib made of pine,
Next thing you know, you would find him in mine.
What fun we had when we were just small,
Taking dad's crutches, we left him to fall.
With his leg in that cast,
Gee Dad....you weren't that fast.
OH, WHAT A RASCAL, THAT BROTHER OF MINE.
Disobeying his mother, he gave it his all.
On the front lawn he yelled, "Just pitch me one ball!"
Shattering the big window, he blamed it on me,
When that baseball hit dad's favorite TV.
Having Kirk around, it never was dull,
If you teased him enough, he'd charge like a bull.
Whether he was roping my feet or throwing bricks at my head,
When I tattled to mom, I got in trouble instead!
OH, WHAT AN ANGEL, THAT BROTHER OF MINE.
The leader of the pack was known as "BIG RED"
All that attention went straight to his head.
Always the one to dish out abuse,
That's how I got the nickname of "MOOSE"!
Campin' and golfin' in Star Valley Sun,
Crashing the golf carts...We had so much fun!
Fishing Old Smokey, so much with our dad,
Those old bear stories were the best times we had.
At Lagoon we could challenge the whole Hercules crew,
Winning the wheelbarrow race was nothing new.
OH, HE WAS MY BUDDY, THAT BROTHER OF MINE.
Lettering in sports was a natural thing,
No matter what he did, Kirk was the King!

Out with the boys, oh the things they would do,
A lot of the stories I can't share with you!
For driving and dating he depended on me,
Kirk had a hard time keeping a license, you see.
In sports and in schoolin', Kirk just had to win,
When he raced my Trans Am, how the tires would spin.
At the Palace we learned to Western Swing,
When it was mastered, he dropped me to do his own thing.
OH, THOSE WERE THE DAYS, WITH THAT BROTHER OF MINE.
He would fix everything with his in-laws and parents,
All of us know of his good intents.
He could build anything whether metal or oak.
If he couldn't fix it, then it wasn't broke!
WHAT A WONDERFUL SON, THAT BROTHER OF MINE.
After being so careful, he found the perfect wife,
To love and to care for, throughout his life.
So proud of Paige as a wife and a mother,
How she cared for his children, as could no other.
He worked far away for quite some time,
Paige managed the home front, being wise with every dime.
Painting came to her as a hobby and talent,
Her crafts are well known, wherever they went.
OH WHAT A HUSBAND, THAT BROTHER OF MINE.
Four little angels were sent from above,
He played and he laughed as he showed them his love.
In the backyard he built, the grandest playhouse,
When it came time for bed, he'd start to rough house.
Campin' and Fishin' daddy took out his boys,
They caught too many fish, even when they made noise!
You could find that daddy in his favorite chair, rocking sweet
Andrea with love and with care.
WHAT A WONDERFUL FATHER, THAT BROTHER OF MINE!
In all of our lives you played a big part,
Though you tried to act tough, you had a huge heart.
Somehow we'll go on, so hard to do,
As the years go by, we'll always remember you!
OH, HOW I'LL MISS THAT BROTHER OF MINE!

I'll be waiting to embrace you, in another place and another time.
Oh, how I Love You, Twin Brother of Mine!
Goodbye for Now, that brother of mine.

After going through so many challenges as a family—my son's cancer, my daughter's adoption and head surgery, my cousin with cancer, and even my husband's ATV accident resulting in a severe head injury, then building our home while living in a camping trailer—you would expect that I was pretty numb at this point. But when my brother took his life, I had no idea how I would survive it. Yes, we had been through some really hard things as a family, but this topped them all.

The reason I tell you this personal and grueling part of my life, is because the only way I got through it was by embracing excellence. Sounds CRAZY, I know! But, here is the deal. When my brother died, he left a wife and four young children. In fact, his daughter was only one. His wife, as you could imagine, was having a horrific time. She was not functioning. So, since we were close and had a great relationship, I began going down to their home, which was about 30 minutes away from me, every other night to sleep over. I would go down, get the kids to bed, sleep, and then get them up and off to school before I would head back to my own home to take care of my own family. This went on for months. It was the only way I knew how to help. Yes, it was extremely hard. It put my brother's death right in my face all the time. But it also made me rise above my own struggles with this. It made me focus outside of myself and be outwardly focused. It required me to dig deep within myself to find strength and the willingness to serve. As I put every ounce of effort into being the best I could be, and strived to help others move forward at the same time, all of us did better. My own family did better as I embraced being in my excellence. I could see the effect it was having everywhere.

At one point, after this had gone on for a long while, I decided it was long enough. I stopped going down to sleep over. I stopped helping as much. I had my own family to care for. I had my own business that needed my attention. What I can tell you is that almost immediately, as soon as I stopped pushing to be in my excellence, I hit rock bottom. I dropped into the deepest depression of my life. I was not even functioning. How could that be?

I am living proof that when we focus on living up to our full potential, we embrace the 7 Traits, and we are willing to live in our excellence—our lives change dramatically. It took everything I could do to turn my life around after my depression. It was in going through my own 7 Traits, that I finally pulled my life back to where it belonged. That is why I teach it to others now.

It took many years, and even more trials, for me to have the courage to share my traits with others. But I am here to tell you that they work. I am thrilled when I see lives change and I see the effect it has in people's lives. I know I was given my challenges to make me stronger. I know that I went through all that I have, in order to share it with the world, and to bless the lives of others.

"Everyone has the power within them to conquer any challenge life throws at them and be stronger because of it!" ~ Kris Barney

TRAIT FIVE:

LIVE in Lasting Love

Limited Love vs Lasting Love

"We all know that LOVE is the greatest power in the Universe, so why are we not taking advantage of using it in all areas of our life? It can be so simple, and yet we make it difficult.

"Stop hating yourself because of what you are not yet. Start loving yourself for what you are right now."

"Your Decisions Today Have the Power to Determine the Outcome of the Rest of Your Life. Will Today Be the Day That Your Decision Becomes Your Defining Moment?"

Chapter 13

Limited Love vs Lasting Love

"Needless to say, you can love people without leading them, but you cannot lead people without loving them." I do know this to be true! ~ John Maxwell

Lasting Love starts with you. You must first unconditionally love yourself. For most people, this can be challenging! But as we put the other six traits into place, this one begins to take shape. Unconditional love is just that—unconditional! For much of this section, I am going to use *unconditional love* as a reference, rather than *lasting love*, until I explain to you the way I look at it.

Love is made up of three unconditional properties, in equal measure:

- Acceptance
- Understanding
- Appreciation

Visualize these three areas being their own side of a triangle. Together the triangle is strong and sound. Remove any one of the three parts, and the triangle falls apart. Think about it—do you really want to live in a world without one of these: acceptance, understanding, or appreciation? Of course we don't! So we need to take a deep look into how our relationships are doing. Are there things in these three areas that might not be in alignment?

I always felt I was good at unconditional love. I loved everyone. I really felt I did. Yet, I never loved me. I was my own worst enemy. It is impossible to love everyone else unconditionally, and not love yourself that way. It starts with you. You must be willing to forgive yourself. Let it go! Yes, easy to say—but perhaps not so easy to do.

Forgiveness is key! When we hold onto hurts, and stay upset with people who have wronged us, we only hurt ourselves. Most of the time, they do not even know or care that we are still in pain, or have feelings of guilt or anger. This whole cycle of holding onto it, is directly hurting you.

We must be forgiving of our own shortcomings, and of others' faults. We all know that nobody is perfect. That means we get to give ourselves a break, as well as everyone else. Unconditional is just that. No conditions! Such as: "I will love myself when I am a size four. I will love myself when I have a new house, or a new car, or a bigger boat, or a better job." These are all conditional, and will never produce genuine love. They might give us temporary happiness—but not true prolonged love of self.

I cannot tell you how many times I thought and even said things like: "I will be happy when I lose 20 pounds," or "I will be happy when my house is organized and completely clean." But guess what? When I lost weight, I didn't find sustained happiness. When the house was all clean and organized—which is more often than it isn't, happiness was not sustained then either. True unconditional love must come from within. Nobody can do this for you. The sooner you learn this one, the better off you will be.

Katy Perry has a huge hit song out titled "Unconditionally." There are several verses in this song with good lessons on unconditional love, but the chorus of it goes like this:

Unconditional, unconditionally
I will love you unconditionally
There is no fear now
Let go and just be free
I will love you unconditionally

When we love unconditionally in all we do, our world changes. We become abundant and we feel real genuine peace. We become free. We stop living in our judgment of ourselves and others. We stop getting upset or being easily offended. We begin to embrace others with their differences and see the value that they bring. We surround ourselves with others and we find happiness and joy in it.

Let's talk about the difference that I see in the two categories I have created. These two categories are Limited Love and Lasting Love. You might want to think of them in terms of conditional love and unconditional love.

Limited Love has several parts. We are talking about having something withheld or held back, perhaps requiring restrictions or expectations to be met in order to receive—"If you do this, I will do that." Restrictions or conditions to our love create limited love. Some examples of this are:

- Discrimination, racism, inequality, prejudice.
- People around you feeling insignificant or unworthy.
- Your child cannot play with a child down the street because they have a different belief system.
- Children feel they are not loved completely if their grades are not high enough.
- Unrealistic expectations.
- A person feels judged by you, even if it is your first time meeting them.
- People feel less-than when they are around you.
- You lack patience with someone.
- Gossip, back biting, being unsupportive, and speaking ill of others.
- A co-worker drives you crazy.
- Jealousy and comparing to others.
- Frustrations and losing your temper.
- Divorce, separation, and splitting up.
- Any form of abuse.

The easiest way to know if you are falling into the trap of limited love is to ask yourself this question: "Will this relationship end with lasting love?" If the answer is no, you are in limited love. You do need to place boundaries around you and your loved ones. You do need to be aware and proactive in protecting yourself from others who are not living in Lasting Love. But you also need to be on high alert to make sure it is not about you being in judgement and falling into the trap.

So what is **Lasting Love**? My best definition is this:

- Love that lasts no matter what.
- Completely unconditional and constant.

- It is something that you not only say, but what you do.
- It is shown through actions, as actions speak louder than words.
- It is given freely, openly, and consistently.
- People feel it from you without even really knowing you.
- Others want to be like you and are not sure why.
- It is found in Sincere Service.
- It is having empathy, humility, honor, sacrifice, and patience.
- It is forgiveness for others and for yourself.
- It is shown through Genuine Gratitude.

Lasting Love is in all aspects of our life—at home and at the office, with our neighbors and friends, and with everyone we encounter. It gets to become a focus where we begin to actually shift our thinking and what goes on in our head. We shift into our heart and come from that space, when we really want to embody Lasting Love.

In breaking down this area with an acronym, I have used the word LIVE, because we really do have to live in Lasting Love. Here is how I break it down:

LIVE in Lasting Love.

L=Learn: We must learn to live this way. Learn the lessons as they come and continue to live this way. Learn from experience. Learn a different way to be. Learn to accept others that are different than you, or have a different opinion than yours. Learn to love yourself with lasting love.

I=Inspire: We get to inspire others to live this way. The more you do it, the more inspiring you are. Be an *example of inspiration as others see you doing this differently. Inspire others to take a stand and be that example as well. Inspire yourself by loving yourself in lasting love.

V=Vigilant: Be Vigilant in your efforts. Be watchful, observant, attentive, alert, and eagle-eyed—on the lookout to spread lasting love, and to put a stop to limited love. Be vigilant in changing how you treat yourself and your relationships.

E=Endless: This is never-ending. It is forever that we get to be continuous in our efforts—constantly improving, always honoring. When we can embrace that this is an endless principle, we can build it for others, and strive to be an example that others follow.

We feel love as we receive it from ourselves and others. But if that feeling does not stay with us always, perhaps we need to look into whether it is conditional or unconditional. Unconditional love is not just a feeling—it is an action. Many times we give unconditional love to others, but we somehow forget to allow ourselves to be loved unconditionally. We must allow ourselves to reap the benefits. It is critical. It will allow you to feel energized and liberated. If you are giving yourself conditional love, you will feel burdened, heavy, overwhelmed, and drained.

We also must learn how to accept unconditional love. This can be hard at times. Our subconscious will go crazy and tell us all kinds of things that are not true, and will try to get us to believe them. The more we love ourselves unconditionally, the more we can love others unconditionally.

Remember the song, "All You Need is Love." There is so much truth in that. Just love everyone. We all need love.

Everyone needs it and deserves it. Be willing to give unconditional love more freely and watch what happens back—you will be more loved. You will actually feel more loved just by loving others. This is a universal truth. What you put out is what you get back, multiplied. So why not just spread unconditional love out there all over everyone? Just think how that would feel as the universe brought it back to you. It really can be that easy!

We are constantly faced with choices. Although it's a wonderful freedom, at times we really struggle making choices. There can be times when it becomes difficult to know our 'right' choice. When those times come, I ask myself a few questions: "What is my purpose and does this align with my purpose?" "What will I gain or lose by making this choice, or that one?" "What am I seeking to accomplish or gain by this choice?"

It always happens without fail, that when I am seeking for good, my choice becomes good and the right one for me. This can mean many different things to each person. I am using this broadly, in the sense that as you seek for good things, you will find them. And when you do, you will have ultimate joy! Ultimate joy comes to us as we serve and do for others. It comes in those times when we seek to have better relationships—when we have a special activity with a loved one, and we feel that whole complete joy of just being with them. There is goodness to be found in all areas. Just look around and search for it.

Seek to find the good in your fellow man. Why would you not choose to seek the good? It amazes me when people only talk about how bad the world is, and how much evil they see out there. Yes, we have a world of turmoil and opposition. But it is unbelievable how much good there is going on every day. There are people going halfway around the world to help and assist others to have things in life that we take for granted. There are fundraisers and non-profit organizations everywhere you look. If you can't find one you like, start your own! There are ways to serve, give, and do for others everywhere. We get to be generous in our giving and in our service.

Be passionate and have a purpose. There are so many good purposes out there. In Scouting, part of their motto is "Do a good turn daily." If everyone in the world lived by this creed, what would our world really be like? Wouldn't that be living in Lasting Love?

If our world had unconditional love for everyone, we wouldn't have war. We wouldn't have law-breaking. We would not have murder. We would not have homelessness. We would not have contention in the workplace. We would not have horrific shootings at public schools or bars or at concerts. We WOULD have love, real freedom, peace, and abundance.

I urge you to seek to know your "Higher Power"—whoever or however that looks for you. Your life will be truly blessed as you do this. I can't even begin to imagine where my life would be if I did not have a huge focus on my Higher Power. Your spirituality is a huge part of you. Nurture it and develop it. Allow it to bless your life. Lasting Love begins with your spiritual connections and values.

"We all know that LOVE is the greatest power in the Universe, so why are we not taking advantage of using it in all areas of our life? It can be so simple, and yet we make it difficult. ~Kris Barney

Chapter 14

Holy Crap! Our Son is Gay!

"We are not held back by the love we didn't receive in the past, but by the love we're not extending in the present."
~Marianne Williamson

It takes much more strength to let go than it does to hang on. Let's talk about Accept and Allow vs Control and Force.

Do you ever wonder why you are not getting the results that you want in your life? Could it be because you are trying to force the results? There is a fine line between allowing and forcing—yet it makes a huge difference in our results. They are polar opposites.

We all know that Love is the greatest power in the universe, so why are we not taking advantage of using it in all areas of our life? It can be so simple, and yet we make it difficult. Accepting and Allowing come from a space of love, which has more power. Sounds too easy, right?

How many times do we go through life trying to Control or Force things? What if I were to tell you that trying to 'Make Things Happen', merely can be causing us to be in resistance. We are getting in our own way.

Accept and Allow vs Control and Force are exactly what we are talking about. Accepting and Allowing are positive and come from a space of love and understanding, where Control and Force are negative and come from a space of conflict and resistance.

When we come from a space of allowing, it creates a positive flow. When we can accept things easily, it creates peace and allows it to feel as if it is our choice. What we focus on is what we get—IT'S TRUE! When we do not accept, it creates the illusion of conflict and resistance. By not allowing, it prevents us from being able to make change. It keeps us stuck.

We get so caught up in our own judgement of ourselves and others. And at times, we are so jaded that we cannot even tell just how much we are turning to Control and Force with everyone around us. What would life look like if we were to actually turn to Accept and Allow?

It takes a lot more courage to let something go, than it does to hang on to it. So what if we were to learn to Accept and Allow and let it go—moving ourselves to a space of Courage? Letting go means accepting what is, exactly as it is, without resistance or even a struggle for control. It is ok to accept things as they are, even if you do not agree with what is happening.

Here is the definition of Acceptance that I found:

1. The act and process of accepting.
2. The state of being accepted or acceptable.
3. Favorable reception; approval.
4. Belief in something; agreement.

When we embrace the definition of Acceptance, there is no room left for Control. To actually let go of the need to control, we must first embrace acceptance. Embracing acceptance is another way of coming from a space of unconditional love. It is remarkable what can happen in our lives when we truly love ourselves and others unconditionally—to let go of Control and allow Love! It is so simple, and yet so profound when you allow it to happen.

"It takes a lot more courage to let something go than it does to hang onto it, trying to make it better. Letting go doesn't mean ignoring a situation. Letting go means accepting what is, exactly as it is, without fear, resistance, or a struggle for control." ~Tyanla Vanzant

The important piece I want to share with you on this is, if you can learn to accept and allow others to be who they are, and to love them unconditionally, rather than try to control and force them to see things your way, you will learn new levels of Lasting Love. If you will embrace a healing heart as you develop this skill, you will shift into complete Lasting Love.

I learned the truth behind this principle with my adult children, as they began making their own choices, no matter what I said or did. Yes, I knew about control and force and accept and allow, but it came into my face in a big way, and I got to really learn what I was made of. I came to a fast realization that I am only in control of me. The only way I would have any influence whatsoever on them, was to live in Lasting Love. It takes determination and a desire to achieve it, at the highest level, but it is worth it. I promise!

Story: The Big Fat Gay Wedding

In our world these days, with so much social media and the ability to put your voice out there, it is easy to hear opinions and arguments on every side of any discussion. It can be easy to have an opinion and voice it—whether we are for or against something. What I want to share with you has been known to get a lot of negative attention, yet I want to share with you our own personal experience of how we chose to do this differently, and what our outcome was because of it.

For a very long time, I have taught that Love is the absence of judgement. Think about this with me, you cannot be in love and judgement at the same time. You must choose the one that is stronger and that you allow yourself to be in. For many people, it is difficult to stay in lasting love almost all the time. This is something I am often challenging clients to do, and to learn how to consciously live it. We must be willing to make a concentrated effort to come from our heart, rather than our head, and stay in unconditional love.

Recently, we had a wedding for my son. It did not look like what I once thought or assumed it would look like. In fact, it was much different. We had a Gay Wedding for my son. I love my son completely. Always have and always will. I love his partner, now his husband, completely, too. Yet for me, our family and our beliefs, or whatever you would call it, the whole Gay wedding just did not fit. For us, we had to DECIDE how we wanted this to look, and how we wanted to CHOOSE to handle it.

For everything that happens in your life, you have to make a decision, and you have to choose how you will act or react to what is going on. By this point in this book, you know well about some of our challenges: my son's cancer—twice, our story of adoption with our daughter, my twin brother's suicide, going through five deaths of close family and friends in two years, and several other things. You also know that it was developing the 7 Traits that got me through those things, and allowed for me to teach you how to do things differently too. Well, this is the same thing. You get to choose how you react!

Because I teach this, I believe that if I am sharing it from the stage and in my book, I surely MUST LIVE IT!! I want to share a post that I posted on Facebook the day before the wedding for thousands to read:

'Tis the day before "Our Big Fat Gay Wedding".....

I started my day quite early—unable to sleep, with lots of thoughts rolling inside my head and emotions running quite high. So I chose to do things a bit differently. I opened up Netflix and there popped up Mamma Mia! (Yes, I have loved this movie and had never been able to get it on Netflix before.)

I watched this movie, all the while, thinking of my own situation. Did I once picture this moment in my head, and it looked different than what reality is coming to be? Absolutely. Has it pushed my buttons? Absolutely. Have I shed tears? Absolutely. Have I questioned if I was strong enough? Absolutely.

But what I can tell you is this...

I ABSOLUTELY and UNCONDITIONALLY love my son, Blake Barney! I have always wanted the best things for him. I have ALWAYS wanted him to find true happiness and love. I have yearned for him to have a family, as this is what he has wanted for many years. I have raised him to be independent, honorable, truthful, brave, loving, kind, dependable, a hard worker, confident, bold, brilliant, strong, committed, true, courageous, and of service to his fellow man. He is all of these things and more, so much more.

I am incredibly PROUD of my son! I am wholeheartedly happy that he has found the love of his life. Does it look different than how I assumed it might look? Yes. But I know that to truly unconditionally love someone, there are always times that it looks a bit different than what you might imagine or assume, for that matter. I am THRILLED to be adding two Amazing Grandchildren to our family, and am excited to be a "parent in law" to Tim. It is a happy day to be adding these wonderful people to our family, and loving and caring for them fully. After all, that is what life is all about, right?

I began today watching a story about a wedding....rather a CELEBRATION of love, family, and happiness. This is what we are creating tomorrow. A CELEBRATION of LOVE. A Unity of FAMILY, full of SUPPORT and HAPPINESS.

What can you expect tomorrow? A HUGE celebration of LOVE and an abundance of HAPPINESS. (Not to mention a gorgeous venue with all the bells and whistles...) We are going to P-A-R-T-Y with the best of them!

Here's to you, Blake & Tim...Let the Games begin!!

Why do I share this with you? Because I have watched so many times, and this is not what happens! I have hundreds of clients or friends, and even strangers, that ask me how I can do this, or tell me stories of their own experience where this is not the case! How sad is that? Even attendees at this wedding could not believe the amount of love and acceptance that was given.

What I want you to know is that living in unconditional love will give you peace. Living in judgement will give you pain. Unconditional love is the absence of judgement. Which one do you want to choose? We really are at choice in how we react to any situation and we create our own outcome. In this situation, we consciously chose to have peace and happiness. To create a loving environment of acceptance and love, and have the greatest party ever!

Here is what our outcome was. I posted this post on Facebook after the wedding, with pictures to show just what we did create:

Our "Big Fat Gay Wedding" was absolutely PERFECT! We were able to Celebrate Love, Unity, and Family.

Yes, we danced down the aisle to begin the party. We had a gay officiator, and a ceremony with their own vows and tears. We had delicious food, a gorgeous venue, an incredible ice sculpture, a gay rainbow wedding cake, a grooms' passionate first dance that turned into "Save a Horse, Ride a Cowboy" country dance, with a full dance floor and everyone screaming the words and dancing to their heart's content. We had a Father's "toast" that he started with an actual piece of toast, a "Surprise" Mother/Groom dance that I had been told would NOT happen—but they surprised me and it was AMAZING. We had tons of our family and close friends come to support us and love on Blake & Tim, and we wrapped up the night with a Bubbles and Sparkler send off.

Many Thanks go out to all our family and friends for their lasting love and support, and to all the troops that traveled from Arizona to be here for Tim & Blake as well! It truly was a Celebration with happiness and love abounding from everywhere. I cannot wait to see all the moments caught on film for our memories to last a lifetime! I LOVE my FAMILY!

As you can see, it was an incredible day and an incredible experience. I know that it could have been so different if we would not have chosen to live this day in unconditional love, and be willing to choose to find the joy in the journey. My challenge for all of us is that we look deep into our hearts and find the love that we deserve to share with others. My hope is that we can all strive to make the choice to live our lives in Lasting Love on a consistent basis, and allow the peace into our lives because of it.

Remember, life is all about our choices and how we choose to live it. Make the decision to live your life in Lasting Love and enjoy your journey—regardless of your circumstances.

"Stop hating yourself because of what you are not yet. Start loving yourself for what you are right now." ~Kris Barney

Chapter 15

What One Sows, One Reaps

"Let today be the day you love yourself enough to no longer just dream of a better life; let today be the day you act upon it." ~Steve Maraboli

Our actions speak louder than our words will ever speak. To actually have these traits change our lives, we must put them into action. As we take dedicated action, our lives flourish. Remember that what we put out there comes back to us multiplied. Take advantage of reaping what you sow.

I am sure you have been thinking about how lasting love relates to your family relationships, friendships, and social situations—and that is good. But how does it relate to your business? Can business issues be resolved better through limited love or lasting love? Most people find it easier to stay in Lasting Love with family relationships. But I want to share with you an experience of how our life was affected by holding a business situation in Lasting Love, and how it resolved a hopeless situation for us.

Story: Love in Business

We had a self-directed ROTH retirement account with a private company, "XYZ, Inc." You make regular contributions, and get to decide where the money is invested. The fund grew substantially over the years.

Then we invested in a start-up company that was going public, and with great enthusiasm we converted the entire investment portfolio into stocks in this new company.

The start-up company failed, and we lost our entire investment of several hundred-thousand dollars! But it didn't end there. We waited and watched for about two years, hoping that something could and would be salvaged from the business. When it became clear there was no hope, we started the process of closing our account with XYZ, Inc. They charged an annual fee based on the perceived value of the portfolio, and the charges were adding up. We sent in the required paperwork to show that the stocks had no value—the company was out of business. We had done everything to properly close our account.

Next, we got a letter from the US Department of Justice telling us that all funds and accounts of XYZ, Inc. were frozen. The owner of the company had been arrested for embezzling $25 million dollars from the company portfolios. Our paperwork had been lost in the chaos and we were stuck paying annual fees on a frozen fund while the company was in receivership. Talk about adding insult to injury! This went on for two years. We were forced to continue paying administration fees each year and an additional cash amount equaling 10% of the perceived value. Even after producing the email correspondence and the proof, we still had to pay out a couple thousand dollars. They would not consider a re-evaluation of the asset because XYZ, Inc. was in receivership.

We were told we could close the account once it had been transferred to a new company (let's call it ABC,

Inc.). Things did not go smoothly with ABC, Inc. either. Their company policy required specific forms in order to close down the account. The start-up company had become insolvent in 2010, and the forms they wanted us to come up with, 6 years later, seemed impossible to produce. We sent in everything we could come up with, but it was not enough to satisfy their policies. They kept asking for more documentation as well as additional fees.

We had reached a boiling point! Meanwhile, the administration fees continued to add up with ABC, Inc. along with a $260 fee to close the account and other fees to review our paperwork. This was getting out of control. We were angry, frustrated, and at our wits' end!

This is where I learned a huge lesson in Lasting Love. I wanted to call these people and read them the riot act—I wanted to scream and yell and make them work with us. I wanted them to see that I was in the right. They were in the wrong, and I should not be punished any further for an employee oversight from the previous company!

My husband said he would handle it. And while I didn't agree with his approach, I let him take it from there. After all, it was entirely in his name and I had no real say anyway.

He approached the situation from a space of Lasting Love. He sat down and wrote them a heartfelt letter expressing gratitude for all the work and effort they put into our account. He told them our whole story from the beginning. He detailed all of the fees we had been forced to pay. He told them of the extreme difficulty of producing the documents they required. He expressed his desire to work with them in any way possible to resolve the situation—added a check for $260—and asked what additional fees he would need to pay. Then he had me mail the envelope. I didn't say much, but I was pretty frustrated with his approach. Especially since he asked me to write out the check!

Here is where I witnessed the power of Lasting Love in a business situation. Four days after mailing the letter and the check, we got an email from ABC, Inc. They thanked us for our patronage, informed us that they had accepted our documentation, and our account was closed. They also said they had waived all fees and they would be returning our check, which we received just a few days later.

Wow! Talk about a monumental shift! It all happened as a result of living in Lasting Love—even in business situations. There is not a stronger force or power than love. And when we live fully in it, it will create amazing results!

"You yourself, as much as anybody in the entire universe, deserve your love and affection." ~Budda

One of the most overlooked, yet profound principles that will open our heart and let Lasting Love take over, is Forgiveness. Yep, I said it. When we can experience forgiveness and allow its power to change us as a person, we become transformed. And when we allow that transformation to occur, we can feel the effect of its healing and embrace the added power and energy it gives to us. We can feel a difference in how we are treating people, rather than reacting to circumstances. We feel more secure in our beliefs, as we embrace them and we are true to ourselves.

So many times we are held back by those things that we have been unwilling to forgive, or even let go of. I remember being so upset with this company who had wronged us repeatedly and continued to cost us money. Yet when my husband chose to handle it differently than I did, it taught me a huge lesson. Then I got to forgive them! Yes, forgive those who hurt you, use you, and take advantage of you. By not forgiving them, you are only hurting yourself! Go through the full process to forgive. And if you do not know how to do that, I suggest that you buy my husband's book. He wrote a book on forgiveness called: *Shine the Light Within—5 Steps to Lighten Your Soul through Forgiveness*. This is not just a shameless plug. It is a fantastic book that will help you a great deal in the area of forgiveness. Hundreds have read it and have been helped by it, and it has not even been out for a year yet. Go to: www.shinethelightwithin.com. Enough said.

As we move through the forgiveness process, we gain more of our power back, and we feel as if a weight has been lifted off of our shoulders. At the same time, it will empower you even more if you will seek for good as you're working through the forgiveness process. Meaning—look for ways to be of sincere service. Find good causes to support and help out. Smile at a stranger and be nice to people at the gas station and the grocery store. As you are putting good out there all around you, you are filling your cup up as much as you are filling theirs.

Story:

A few years ago, my daughter—who is the 'baby' of our family—was off to college for her first year away from home. She had completed a full semester and was doing really well. She was actually very smart and had earned a leadership scholarship for college. She had been very good at getting good grades, was very diversified with skills and talents, and was just pretty much exceptional. Of course, I may be a bit biased. When she came home for Christmas break, we had a wonderful time.

She headed back to college the first week of January, and two weeks later, she was in a pretty horrific car accident. The accident was not her fault. But she was in the wrong by not wearing her seat belt. Her car was totaled and she had a severe head injury. Long story short, we tried everything we could to keep her at college, to keep her scholarship, and to get her well at the same time—but it didn't work. Her head injury was bad enough that she had no short term memory. She could not even remember her classes or what building they were in, or any of the content to try and take a final exam. She would get lost driving around the small town and would even lose her car—her new car, since the other one was totaled. She would forget what color it was, etc. Anyway, after weeks of grueling with the challenges, we finally had to bring her home and withdraw her from school, as we nursed her back to health.

With head injuries, the side effects are pretty horrible. She changed so much, it was like she wasn't the same person. It was hard as a parent to go through this with her, but harder for her as it changed everything in her world. It changed her friends. It changed her emotionally and physically, and put her on a completely different path.

The reason I tell you part of this story is that this was a huge ordeal for me to be able to forgive. I had to forgive her for not wearing a seatbelt. I had to forgive the boy that hit her. I had to forgive many consequences of the reality of what this did to her. It was not easy to forgive all of this. This was my princess! This was the child that was the hardest for us to get. And her entire world was changed in an instant.

I would be lying if I told you forgiving was easy. I would be lying if I said there are not still times that I have to go back and forgive even now. Her life is not the same, and honestly mine is not either. But when I am willing to forgive, willing to love with all my heart, and willing to live in lasting love, our lives are unbelievable! Does her life right now look like I once thought it would? No. Is she happy, yes. And that makes me happy. Does my life right now look how I thought it would? No. But what I can tell you is that it is better than ever! It is a fantastic life with a loving caring family. We are all close, and we love spending time together making memories that bind.

You can do this. You have it in you. You can live your life in Lasting Love and you will be happy you did!

"Your Decisions Today Have the Power to Determine the Outcome of the Rest of Your Life. Will Today Be the Day That Your Decision Becomes Your Defining Moment?" ~Kris Barney

TRAIT SIX:

CONNECT in Complete Communication

Confusing Communication vs Complete Communication

"Communication is like a backbone. It is required if we want to be successful!"

"I have found that we create our reality. And when we recognize what we are doing, and make the corrections needed—we can be happier, healthier, and more successful!"

"Good Communication is so much more than just words—it is our actions and our ability to listen. It is communicating clearly and being understood."

"Effective Communication begins and ends with intentional listening.

Chapter 16

Confusing Communication vs Complete Communication

"Communication is a skill that you can learn. It's like riding a bicycle or typing. If you're willing to work at it, you can rapidly improve the quality of every part of your life." ~Brian Tracy.

Story: The Olympic Massage

My husband and I attended a gorgeous three-day-weekend conference retreat. The facilitator explained our next communication exercise. He turned the lights down low, and had us sit on a pillow facing each other to prepare for an intimate experience. My husband's instructions were to give me a hand massage. My instructions were to communicate how I would like that massage to be done. At the time of this conference, we had been married for 32 years. I knew my husband already had a pretty good idea of how I would want him to massage my hand. We had this in the bag!

The facilitator said, "Begin."

My husband, being the light-hearted jokester that he is, went at this massage with vigor. He aggressively lathered up my hand with lotion and began rubbing it as if he was trying out for the deep tissue massage Olympics!

I immediately went into my head thinking, "What in the heck are you doing? You know I have neuropathy and pins and needles in my hands. How dare you hurt me! After 32 years of marriage, you know this!" I did not say a word. The more he rubbed, the madder I got! He was like a little boy in the candy store. He was on a mission. He was going to do it the wrong way until I communicated how I wanted it to be done. He was pushing my buttons all the way in!

All the other couples were having this fantastic moment of connection and communication. But for me, this was a disaster! I blamed him. This was entirely his fault. Yet, I was the one that did not communicate. I was the one who assumed he would know what I wanted him to do. I was the one who was out of alignment with what we had been instructed from the facilitator.

Has anything like this happened to you? Have you had a Lack of Communication Moment? This exercise was great for me. Although we have a fabulous marriage and never really felt we had communication issues, it helped us realize how easily we can fall into the trap of getting into our own head, while failing to use the knowledge and skills we have. Lack of communication happens all the time, all day long! Every day! Even when you are not sitting on pillows, in dim lighting, with the one you love!

"Communication is like a backbone. It is required if we want to be successful!" ~Kris Barney

Successful leadership requires excellent communication skills. Remarkable relationships require excellent communication skills. Effective managing, teamwork, and parenting require excellent communication skills.

Good communication is an essential key to be effective in relationships of all types—such as teams at work, members of a board, community events, successful parenting, and even in our significant relationships. It will solve problems in the workplace, bring people closer both at work and at home, it will increase our engagement with each other, and foster a sense of belonging. Since communication effects literally every aspect of our lives, isn't it time to take a deeper look at just how excellent your skills really are?

Communication should rate very high on your list of skills to be conquered. Our communication affects us every day, and in every situation. Communication done well can assist us to avoid conflicts and misunderstandings, while building trust, increasing productivity, and successfully engaging with one another. This has a huge impact in the workforce—but also imagine how this would affect you in your personal life.

I speak and train on *Communication from the Inside Out* with Corporations, Associations, and even personal coaching clients. And believe it or not, I almost always start with communication basics. What I have learned is that most communication problems start by our not knowing or following basic principles—and they expand from there. In our society, having so much technology has caused our communication skills to deteriorate. We are losing some of our human connection, and we are getting used to 'out of context' emotional communication through texting or emails. Because of this, we are also losing our natural ability to communicate through body language, voice inflection, tone, eye contact, touch, and even listening. These skills are needed and necessary to communicate effectively and precisely. The other huge issue we have with communication is that we allow ego and emotion to take over. Once ego or emotion gets involved in communication, your skill level just flies out the window.

Let's focus on the foundational areas that will give you instant success in improving your communication skills. A huge key here is to assess where you are personally. Take an honest look, and take action to create improvement.

We are going to talk about two types of Communication: Confusing Communication and Complete Communication.

Confusing Communication is any type of communication with an unclear message or a negative message, either during the conversation, or when the conversation is over. It can be when things are unclear, questionable, or upsetting. There is judgment and harshness, as well as the silent treatment. You may feel you have no voice or you are not using your voice. Or it can be a feeling of not being heard, whether that is self-inflicted or you feel intimidated and like you are not allowed to share how you feel. Or if you do speak up, you may feel that it is falling on deaf ears, and you are treated as though you were not heard and it did not matter. It can occur when you are spoken to, rather than spoken with. No one likes to be spoken down to or belittled by someone who is taking advantage of an authority position. Consider how it might be affecting you in your relationships, your job, or your business—and even with your effectiveness and productivity. Confusing Communication comes from things like:

- Not speaking up for yourself
- Not speaking your truth
- Finding fault with the other person
- Jumping to conclusions
- Lack of personal integrity
- Having unrealistic expectations
- Being in judgement
- Not paying attention to body language, voice inflection, and attitude
- Playing the blame game
- Being dishonest, even just a little white lie
- Not taking accountability
- Not interested in the other person
- Putting yourself first, rather than putting others first
- Not being respectful
- Being impatient
- Being irresponsible
- Poor listening skills
- Uninterested in the conversation or project
- Misinterpreting conflict or sensing avoidance

That is quite a list, yet it's just a drop in the bucket. Many of the effects of Confusing Communication come down to having negative emotions, or negative ways of being involved at the time of the conversation. How often do we allow negativity to come into play in our everyday conversations, as well as in our very important moments? Confusing Communication also happens when we are allowing distractions in, while attempting to communicate and multi-task at the same time. Now I am all about efficiency, multi-tasking, and being productive. Yet we also must be proactive in controlling our emotions, determining our focus, and managing our communication in a way that is beneficial for all parties involved.

Complete Communication involves clarity, focus, and listening—all going on at the same time. It requires us to be non-judgmental and filled with genuine concern and interest in what others have to say. It is about LISTENING completely, and not trying to come up with our answer or opinion before they are even through with their statement. It comes from your heart. It comes from living positive traits, and having genuine concern for other people. It involves putting into place and living good values, as well as being conscious of our actions, and alert to the ways we can improve. It is created when true respect is given to others and a priority is put on creating a way to communicate better. It happens when we allow feedback without taking it personal, when we create a safe and friendly space, when we allow understanding to be a big focus as well as empathy skills, and allow thoughtfulness to be included in our communication.

Complete Communication comes from:

- High level of Integrity
- Courageous Confidence
- Be Interested
- Be Accountable
- Keep your word

- Hold yourself and others to a higher standard
- Be open and willing to listen
- Nurturing and effective in your skills
- Be accepting and non-judgmental
- Be observant and aware of body language
- Be aware of what is going on
- Be accepting of responsible feedback
- Find clarity and confirm what you heard
- Create a friendly safe space
- Use empathy and thought skills
- Good listening skills, with focus on what is being said
- Taking personal accountability and responsibility for your communication
- Be filled with Lasting Love (Unconditional Love)

And that is just for starters! As we up-level our lives, our communication levels improve. As we work on our personal development and awareness, our communication skills improve. As we raise our love for others and ourselves, our communication skills improve. As we up-level our empathy skills and our gratitude, we become better communicators.

I love to use the acronym CONNECT with Concise Communication, because if we are not connecting, we are really not communicating. Here is what I train on:

CONNECT in Complete Communication

C=Clarity: Be clear in your communication. Ask for clarity if you are not sure. Speak your truth. Defend your side without emotion or ego. Find clarity and confirm what you heard. Be clear and concise whenever possible in your communication. And ask for clarity if you feel you do not understand what they meant or how it was meant.

Observe: Observe and be willing to see things from their perspective. Find common ground and create connection. Observe and watch body language, voice inflection, eyes, and hands. Observe how well you are listening, and recognize when you check out.

Nourish: Nourish and find ways to communicate without face-to-face or touch. Follow up with people in nonverbal communication. Nourish your network and make connections.

Navigate: Find and create a way to make your communication work better. Be willing to try new ways to learn. Navigate ways for your teams at work and your relationships outside of work, to communicate better with consistency and respect.

Effective: Be effective with communication. Find your faults and improve your skills. Be aware and focus on your abilities—both good and bad. Make adjustments and be willing to take a look at how effective your skills in communication are.

Considerate: Be considerate. Care about who you are having communication with. Be courteous and patient. Be consistent and confirm what you heard. Being considerate means giving the other person the benefit of the doubt—before you get emotional and upset with them.

Train: Train yourself to LISTEN. Become a better listener. Train yourself to do it better. Train others how to communicate better with you. Train your team how to communicate better and improve their skills. Train your family and loved ones how to interact and communicate completely. Train yourself and others to be responsible in their communication.

"Communication—the human connection—is the key to personal and career success." ~Paul Meyer.

Communication makes all the difference in the world for us, both personally and professionally. Connection will improve our communication on all levels—it will make us more successful, and keep us happy!

Let me repeat the statement from the beginning of this section::

Successful Leadership requires excellent communication skills. Remarkable Relationships require excellent communication skills. Effective Managing, Teamwork, and Parenting require excellent communication skills. How do you rate your skill level at this point?

I want to share three foundational factors in Communication for you to consider, and perhaps ponder how they show up in your life.

#1. Clear Communication.

In my story with my husband, you just heard what not to do, right? We must let go of assumptions and expectations. We also must use our words! People are 100% better at understanding words and actions, than they are at reading minds!

In high school I played basketball. Our team went to state. The key factor to our team doing so well was a coach who knew great communication skills. The coach learned our talents and abilities, placed us in a position to take full advantage of those skills, and built offensive plays that capitalized on those skills. He then taught us to communicate together as a team to have the best success. We learned all kinds of skills to communicate in both verbal and nonverbal ways, and it paid off immensely.

I knew, as a left forward, that when the point guard called switch, I was running over to the right side and popping out to put up a baseline shot. The coach knew I was consistent at hitting that shot. Our coach knew each of our talents and abilities, and knew how to capitalize on them, and taught us how to communicate as a team to be more effective. Thus, we won more games, and outplayed our competition.

Are you capitalizing on the skills and abilities of the teams in your life? This could be your family, your executive team at the office, or perhaps your personal assistant, graphic artist, and web designer. Are you having clear communication? Do you have regular opportunities to discuss how to improve communication?

#2. Complete Connection

At a young age, I was taught to STOP, LOOK, and LISTEN. Back then, it was for safety. But I want you to think about this—don't we need to Stop, Look, and Listen in our communication?

Listening is a skill. In our society, we are losing this skill. There are too many distractions—we are too busy and overstimulated. Technology has increased our ability to reach more people faster, while getting much worse at our communication skills. Yet, people need to be heard. It is an absolute human need! Let's look at social media.

Do we hear more positive or more negative input? Is it real communication or is it just noise? The biggest communication problem our society faces right now is that we listen to reply, rather than to understand. It's true!

There are studies that show only 7% of communication is verbal; 38% is tone and inflection; and 55% is in our body language. I am not sure that this study is completely accurate, but I do know that we have more nonverbal communication in every conversation we have. It is important enough that you should be paying attention to it. Are you even aware of your body language? Are you open and approachable, or closed-off and stern? Are you welcoming and creating complete connections? How is your communication coming across? Are you recognizing what others are feeling during and after they are in a conversation with you?

WIIFM? Everyone wants to know, "What's in it for me?" Consider this: What's in it for them? WIIFT? What's in it for them to be in a relationship with you? When we raise the bar and show others, through communication and teamwork, that it is a different experience working with us—it attracts more clients, and we will retain more clients and employees. Our relationships become lasting and meaningful in all aspects of our lives! What's in it for them to be in a relationship with you?

#3. Constant Consideration

Everyone needs to belong. It is a physical, emotional, and spiritual need. We all need to belong in all aspects of our life—in our family, our community, and with our self. This is a proven concept with Maslow's Hierarchy of needs, along with several others. As we feel that we belong, we begin to feel how we are considered.

Story: A Plate of Cookies

It was a Saturday at noon. I was still in my pajamas, with a serious case of bed head and yesterday's mascara now much lower on my face. I was in my back office writing my book. It was the first Saturday in six weeks that I had not been out of town speaking, or had other obligations. The doorbell rang. NOT the front doorbell, but the back doorbell! That meant someone was standing at the glass doors looking right into the kitchen, which was the room next to mine. There was nowhere to go without being seen, and I was the only one home! So I did what any sane person would do—I stood up and peeked out the blinds to see if I knew who it was! I did not recognize the truck in my driveway! So I fluffed my bedhead, rubbed the mascara from under my eyes, and went to answer the door.

There stood a teenage girl with a plate of cookies. I opened the door and she said, "The youth group in our area are spreading the love today, and we thought of you!" I immediately felt valued, respected, recognized, and that ahhhh moment! How would this make you feel?

It was a moment of communication in which I felt loved, cared about, and considered. Isn't that what we all want to feel? Again, one of our basic needs according to Maslow and his hierarchy of needs, is to belong. Belonging is huge!! How often are you making others feel they belong through your communication, and how often are you creating those "ahhhh" moments for others? Are you doing things that are unexpected? Are you recognizing others and giving compliments, or a pat on the back? Are you good at managing expectations in your workplace and at home in your relationships? Are you creating an environment in which others feel they belong?

Constant Consideration will immediately add value to all relationships! Complete Connection will enhance your influence and create deeper connection. Clear Communication will assist you in capitalizing on your abilities and creating a more effective team—thus being more effective and more productive. Isn't that what we all want anyway?

Good communication and teamwork are a choice. You decide how you will show up!

"I have found that we create our reality. And when we recognize what we are doing, and make the corrections needed, we can be happier, healthier, and more successful!"
~Kris Barney

Chapter 17

The Power in Good Communication

"Your ability to communicate is an important tool in your pursuit of your goals, whether it is with your family, your co-workers or your clients and customers." ~Les Brown

All good relationships begin with good communication. I cannot stress this enough. In our lives, we have hundreds—if not thousands—of relationships. And the only way to stay aligned and calm with them all, is if we are able to communicate completely and clearly. It is a true sign of wisdom when you choose to learn great communication skills, and a valuable characteristic when you can respond calmly and peacefully when someone is responding to you negatively. This is a skill that is not easily mastered, but can be profound, and shows a level of control beyond what most people can or are willing to achieve.

Communication works well for those who master it, and are willing to work at it. We should take advantage of the opportunities that we have to practice our communication skills, and be willing to learn how to communicate better. It is interesting to me that in our corporate world, communication is considered a soft skill. Yet, in reality, it is one of the most valuable skills you can possess. It can assist you to advance in your career, mitigate conflict, improve relationships, and allows you to be more productive and effective in all aspects of your life.

When we have good strong communication, we are powerful. To achieve this power and influence, it takes others being able to trust you. Trust is so important—in fact, Steven Covey said this:

"Trust is the glue of life. It's the most essential ingredient in effective communication. It's the foundational principle that holds all relationships."

Trust is essential. Think about it—do you even want to be in a conversation, let alone a relationship, with someone that you do not trust? When we do not trust someone, we do not respect them. When we do not respect them, we do not value them. It is pretty hard to have a good relationship with someone when you feel that you cannot trust, respect, or value them.

No one wants to be around that 'I'm better than you are' executive or a condescending supervisor. We do not appreciate a micromanager, or even an unsympathetic manager. For us to appreciate those in a leadership position, we want to be able to be respected and honored—not belittled or talked down to. This is important to remember if you are in a leadership position. It is also important to remember if you are the employee, as people are more likely to treat you with respect when you show respect. People honor those who live up to their beliefs and values. As we all put our best foot forward, we are more likely to have valuable communication, and have less drama and fewer consequences from poor communication skills.

Communication is more than just talking with people—it is about connection. In our world right now, people are starving for connection. Because of technology, we are having a crisis in our communication and in our need for connection and interaction with other people. One of the biggest benefits of good communication at work, is that we are more engaged as co-workers or even as employees. We feel that we belong and, in turn, take more ownership in aligning with the beliefs, goals, or even objectives of the company. This is even true in our family dynamics, for that matter. When we feel needed and heard, we feel valued and appreciated. We have an increase in self-confidence, and are more committed to a relationship or even a team.

When we have good communication, it will improve employee engagement and retention. People feel valued and, in turn, want to remain at their job. When employees are taught tools and skills to communicate better, they are more productive and more successful. It can almost completely eliminate conflict when you have good communication. And you no longer have to have someone mitigating the conflict. It removes many of the misunderstandings, and even the feeling of being misunderstood. It allows us to own our power, and feel more confident in communicating what we mean. It also allows us to become better at clear communication in the first place. There are valuable communication patterns, and when we are communicating clearly, we can easily make those adjustments necessary to avoid being misunderstood. When we train our entire team together, we can all be on the same page—and it is proven to be much more successful.

Effective communication will raise productivity, and can assist us in avoiding various disasters that can happen in business. It can save time and effort on all sides of the equation. It can create better relationships between managers and leaders, and will raise the level of respect for everyone when you communicate more effectively.

Imagine the improvement in customer service, if communication techniques and tools were taught. The customer would feel understood, and the employee would not feel the pressure and stress of the disgruntled customer. The stress levels would be much more manageable when an employee feels they have the skills necessary to handle any situation. This is very empowering. They can assist the customer to feel understood, be more accepting of the situation, and give feedback and information in a way that the client will be much more likely to receive.

When we have good communication in the workplace, we are more productive. People are more likely to show their talents and abilities, because it is a safe space. They are much more likely to take that risk, and make a suggestion or comment that could be very valuable. Employee engagement is a significant aspect of employee productivity. And let's face it—we all benefit when we have a more productive team. When we understand the talents and abilities of our team, and our team feels safe and understood, it is incredible what can transpire.

Connection is such a huge piece in our communication, and is a need that we all have. When the right communication is going on, it becomes incredible to watch how well a team can focus and create together. When everyone is doing their part, and the team works like a well oiled machine—production skyrockets. Understanding communication gives a leader more information about their employees that they would have otherwise overlooked. This insight lets the leader make strategic decisions on delegation, employee development, team development, and strategic ways to drive business success and productivity.

I like how Jim Rohn put this:

"If you just communicate, you can get by. But if you communicate skillfully, you can work miracles."

Good communication is not just about being able to accurately and precisely present ideas, or even information. It is not just about mitigating conflict. Communication is a huge part of our sales, customer service, client relationships, and our company culture and community. It's wrapped up in our employee engagement, our teams skills and dynamics, and even gets involved in our ability to be innovative. It is crucial that we have the skills and abilities to communicate more effectively. Employees are craving engagement and community, and want a strong company culture. To have employee retention, we must be willing to do what it takes to fulfill the need for good communication.

Here are some ways to improve communication for you to consider:

- Listen to your team members
- Increase face-to-face interaction
- Ask for employee opinions
- Let employees have a vested interest
- Leverage your digital teams
- Have honest feedback & allow anonymous feedback
- Hold regular one-on-one meetings
- Admit it when you are wrong
- Have high integrity and accountability
- Create a safe environment

- Share ideas and value others' opinions
- Teach tools and communication skills
- Have group collaboration
- Create fun activities and team building games

When it is all said and done, all of the things listed above will assist in creating good communication in the workplace and in the home. When it is a focus and a priority, it becomes a good habit that we value and appreciate—which, in turn, we will do. Maintain open lines of communication and continually work to develop a higher standard of communication.

"Good Communication is so much more than just words—it is our actions and our ability to listen. It is communicating clearly and being understood." ~Kris Barney

Chapter 18

Are You Really Listening?

"The biggest communication problem is we do not listen to understand. We listen to reply." ~Zig Ziglar

I've heard it said that the most important thing in communication is hearing and understanding what isn't actually being said. This refers back to verbal and nonverbal communication. Many years ago, Professor Mehrabian combined the statistical results of two studies and came up with the now famous—and famously misused—rule that communication is only 7% verbal, and 93% non-verbal. The nonverbal component was made up of body language (55 percent) and tone and inflection of voice (38 percent). Our verbal use of communication is the lowest level of the communication spectrum, which that makes our outside communication, or nonverbal communication, very powerful.

Let's talk about these nonverbal cues. First is Body Language. Are you aware of your own body language? Whether we want to admit it or not, we are instinctively aware of body language when others are speaking to us. We instinctively know if they are upset, angry, or just frustrated with us. We can easily tell signs in another person's body language, without even having any real training in this area. We are very intuitive and are extremely aware of people and the way their body language 'speaks' to us.

Several years ago, I took a lot of classes on body language and how to read body language. It was quite exciting and fun. I could watch others and have an entirely different conversation going on, just by watching their hands, their legs and feet, as well as their facial expressions, and their use of their eyes. I remember watching one of my children, and being very accurate on telling whether this child was telling me the truth, or if I was being lied to. I could also be very accurate on integrity and principles of people in reading body language at networking events and social activities. There really is a whole world out there all about body language and nonverbal communication.

The important part for you is to be aware of it. Years ago, they taught all kinds of techniques about mirroring the person interviewing with you, or even ways to manipulate others and get them to trust you so that they would buy from you, or that you would be able to manipulate them into getting what you want out of them. I do not agree with this technique at all and, for the most part, there has been a great uprising against it. People hate to be manipulated and persuaded in communication, and that is not what I want you to focus on. In fact, I would rather you stayed as far away from that part of communication as possible.

Effective body language encourages others that it is safe to share, and is an additional part of communication that is very valuable. It helps you to know when someone has basically 'left' the conversation and is no longer interested. Or it helps you recognize when someone shows nervousness in their legs and feet, and are not strong and powerfully rooted in their foundation. If you have the opportunity to learn body language, and are using it to be a better communicator—Great! It can be very valuable for a leader of a group, or a person of influence, and can assist you in being a better communicator. But formal training is not required to be more assertive and watch what is going on when someone is speaking. You can easily see when someone is not being truthful, and you can learn to watch someone to see what their normal is, and then watch as they begin to squirm or get uneasy.

Body language is not just used for the negative. Watch a person when they have exciting news—watch how their eyes are wide open and they share eye to eye contact with you. What happens when your significant other looks you in the eyes? What is that saying to you? I know for me, I can read my husband's eyes pretty accurately, and can tell a lot of his emotions even before words are spoken. As you practice being more aware of body language, you will begin to pick up on different gestures and movements that will clue you in much more, as to what is going on in someone's mind—without them saying a word.

Besides body language, there is also tone and inflection. Tone and inflection are pretty easy to detect quickly, and can also alert you as to what is going on. We can hear fear, excitement, anger, shyness, happiness, laughter, and even tears. We can hear the emotions going on in others, which gives us a lot of information for us to consider in our communication. On the flip side of this, as we are communicating with others, we must be aware of our own tone and inflection—especially in the workplace. No one enjoys being talked down to, or belittled, even by a condescending tone or inflection. No one wants to have someone mad or angry with them. No one wants to be yelled at or put down. And I feel that no one should be treated this way. It is only those who do not have good communication skills that will allow themselves to stoop to a negative level of communication. Tone and inflection are powerful and are crucial to good communication skills. If you find yourself in a situation where you do not feel you have mastered this area, make it a conscious effort to improve. It takes work and skill to be a good communicator, but it can easily be learned and adapted into your life.

"The quality of your Communication is the quality of your life."
~Tony Robbins

My question for you is this: What is the quality of your communication?

I would like you to think about your favorite leaders, or the people you respect at the highest levels. Are they good in their communication? Why? What I have found is that most great leaders are great communicators and they have one huge thing in common—they LISTEN.

Listening has become a lost art in our world. I love how Zig Ziglar said,

"The biggest communication problem is we do not listen to understand. We listen to reply."

There is so much truth in this! We are so busy thinking of our next response to someone that we do not even hear what they are telling us. There are all kinds of studies out there with proof of how significant this is in our world right now

Hearing is accidental, involuntary, and effortless. Listening is focused, voluntary, and intentional. When was the last time that you listened intentionally, being focused and very involved in listening to what they are actually talking about? We have gotten so conditioned as a society with all kinds of noise in our lives, that we pretty much tone out.

To be a good listener, we must be interested in what other people have to say. I learned this thirty years ago from the book, *How to Win Friends and Influence People*. The rules remain the same. We should think of questions we can ask the other person about them, rather than speaking about ourselves first. How great would it be if everyone really actually wanted to know about you, and asked you a couple of questions about yourself, rather than just immediately start talking all about themselves? This technique really does influence people in a positive way. You are showing consideration and interest in what they have to say and in who they are. It opens up the door for trust and respect, and allows you to listen and get to know what they have to say. It bridges the gaps that we can have in our communication, and embodies empathy and understanding. When we use this technique, we are able to know others better, be more influential, and create a space of true connection.

Being married for 35 years, we have had our share of great communication, as well as some pretty lousy communication. And raising children is always fun in those teenage years when communication becomes somewhat awkward or difficult. Yet when I truly listened and ask good questions, we were able to have phenomenal communication. It really does work. Our best communication is when it is intentional. It is when it is decisive rather than distracted, and when it is intentional and interested.

Being a great listener is a valuable trait. It will take you to greater levels in your job, and will create unbelievable relationships in your life. If you want to achieve more—listen better. If you want a promotion—learn to be a good listener. If you want others to know you care—Be a better Listener!

"Effective Communication begins and ends with intentional listening." ~Kris Barney

TRAIT SEVEN:

IMPLEMENT Impeccable Integrity

Inconsistent Integrity vs Impeccable Integrity

"Integrity is doing what is right always—not what is simply easier."

"Influence comes through your example of being ethical and full of integrity in all that you do."

"Highest Standards & Honorable Character are your best Assets. Yet isn't that just good Ethics?"

"Exceptional character creates noteworthy performance and the highest professionalism."

Chapter 19

Inconsistent Integrity or Impeccable Integrity

"Real Integrity is doing the right thing, knowing that nobody's going to know whether you did it or not." ~Oprah Winfrey

Integrity is choosing your thoughts and actions based on values and beliefs, rather than personal gain.

What does Impeccable Integrity mean to you? What value do you place on yourself? Your personal value is determined by several factors—one of the most important is your personal integrity. As I have contemplated the trait of Impeccable Integrity, I've concluded that this important trait is not considered as important as it used to be. Is your word your bond? Do you keep the commitments you make to others, or do you say you will be someplace when you really have no intention of showing up?

Your personal value is determined by several contributing factors, one of the biggest and most important is your personal integrity. My question for you is this: "Do you feel you have Impeccable Integrity?

I am going to challenge you on this one, and possibly even challenge your beliefs. I encourage you to take a look within, and determine where you could up your integrity. I have spoken to and trained thousands of people on integrity, and I have pushed thousands of buttons. But that's okay, if it causes people to take a look at where they are and where they could improve. I work on improving my integrity every single day. I do not push your buttons to see if I can tick you off, but rather to see if I can get your attention and challenge you to take a look at this, even if it is a bit different than how you have looked at it before. My intention here is for you to up-level your life. And the best way to do that is to actually notice where you are out of balance or out of alignment in your life.

Here are some of the definitions of integrity, according to Wikipedia: Integrity is a concept of consistency of actions, values, methods, measures, principles, expectations, and outcomes. In ethics, integrity is regarded as the honesty and truthfulness or accuracy of one's actions. Integrity is the inner sense of wholeness deriving from qualities such as honesty and consistency of character. As such, one may judge that others 'have integrity' to the extent that they act according to the values, beliefs, and principles they claim to hold.

Allow me to give you a couple of examples and even some data. I will start with a simple alarm clock or the alarm on your phone. Do you hit the snooze button? This is a real question. Do you hit the snooze button to grab a few more minutes before you really have to wake up or get out of bed? If you do, I would like you to assess what this might mean for you. There are several things that this simple, yet profound act signifies, especially if you hit it more than once. First, it means that you had no intention of getting up when it went off, and that you do not feel that you need to complete things the first time you are asked or told—whether by yourself or with others. Second, it signifies that you do not need to trust yourself, as you will have second chances in life. Third, it shows that you allow yourself to show up late, possibly miss deadlines, have second or even third chances, and that you will allot extra time if you really want it. I go into this concept quite a bit in a video on YouTube or on my blog. I also use it as a demonstration with live audiences. It is interesting how accurate it is. It has a direct correlation to our subconscious and to our personal integrity, and what we tell ourselves and the actions that we take.

I have used this snooze button scenario at corporate trainings, breakout sessions, conferences, multiple day events, and even retreats. Across the board, our numbers and percentages have been almost identical, when it came to the people using a snooze button and their results. It is astounding to see how many filed extensions for their taxes, asked for a little more time on a deadline, showed up late to work or meetings—even the most important ones. We have had high percentages that relied on second chances and extended opportunities. I am sure you are getting this picture. I could go into all the details on how this is actually very bad for you and your sleeping patterns, and how it actually takes away the effects of the quality of sleep that you did get—but my point is that it is not serving you. My advice to you is STOP IT.

There are times that we all justify the things that we do in our lives. In fact, many times we even place blame on others as to why we do things, like, "It is my parents fault, the entire time we were growing up we had blah, blah, blah." We must take accountability of our life if we want it to change.

What is your integrity worth to you?

I was at a gas station one day, and decided I wanted a Diet Coke. Now impeccable integrity would have been to have water, as health is important to me. But stay with me here for a minute. There was a man in front of me. He pulled out a new cup and poured himself a drink. I got my drink as well and followed him to the counter. As the man got up to the cashier, she asked him, "Is that a new cup or a refill?" He said, "Oh, it's a refill." FORTY CENTS! His integrity was worth forty cents!! Where are you forty cents out of alignment with your personal integrity? Are you selling yourself short?

If the scales of justice were measured in your life, how would they look? Would they be balanced, or would they be tipped to one side or the other? Do you make sure that you give back the extra change that the cashier gave you by mistake? Do you find the owner of the wallet you found, with all the money still inside? Do you pay for a new cup at the gas station or do you say it is a refill? Do you return items to the store after using them or even wearing them? Do you sell yourself short when you could be empowering yourself through your integrity?

I know this is a harsh look into our core, but isn't being honest and having integrity something we all want? How would it feel to live in a world where EVERYONE KEPT THEIR WORD or everyone had stalwart integrity? We would not have to lock our doors. Everyone would keep their word. Everyone would pay their bills on time and not miss payments. There would not be robberies at all. Embezzlement would end. Lying and cheating would not exist. Could you even imagine a world like this?-

I want to share some statistics with you. This is not a new study. I am sure the numbers are now even greater., and yet it still was unbelievable to me:

- The average iPod or smartphone has $800+ in pirated music downloaded on it.
- 95% of music downloaded is illegal.
- 42% of software running in the world was illegally downloaded.
- $2.7 billion dollars in workers' earnings are lost each year due to online piracy.

Those are just a few items I found. I know that this goes on, but we do not need to be contributors! There is honor in keeping our word, in having integrity at all times and in being different from everyone else. It really does matter!

I love this quote by Oprah Winfrey:

"Real integrity is doing the right thing, knowing that nobody's going to know whether you did it or not."

Impeccable Integrity starts with you! You must first have integrity with yourself before you will ever have it with others. Wisdom is knowing the right thing to do. Integrity is doing it.

If I haven't pushed your buttons yet, my last question for you might. "Do you drive five miles or more over the speed limit?" I am serious about you answering this question. It is very rare that anyone in the room does not go at least five miles over the speed limit. We are going to imagine that you said yes. I also am going to assume that you are in a 55-mile-per-hour or higher area. So doing the math, that would put you out of alignment by 10% of the speed limit. Now, because I am nice, I will give you the benefit of the doubt and say you are only 5% out of alignment. You are only 5% out of alignment with obeying the law of the land!

This is not about me being the speed police. In fact, my first car was a Trans Am, and was a very fast car. I do like to go fast in my cars. This is probably one of the areas that I have to continually work to keep it in alignment! But this is about being in complete integrity, which also includes obeying the law completely. Do they tell us we can obey only 95% of the laws of the land, and that we can choose which 5% of the laws we want to disobey? I know that you will not get a ticket for going only five over. That is not my point. That is pure and total justification. We can all justify anything we want to do if that is what we want. If you are finding yourself having to justify anything in your life, you should take a look deeper into what is really going on. But, back to our speeding scenario, would you want your neighbors to choose which 5% of the laws of the land they do not obey? Maybe your child's school teacher, which laws can they not obey?

Seriously, all our neighbors and people out there are doing this, and justifying why it works for them. I just want you to look at you. Where else are you just 5% out of alignment? That is what I am talking about. What are you beginning to notice? Where else are there slight changes that have significant consequences? Let's look at airplanes. If the captain of the airplane started his takeoff and programed in the coordinates for the location you wished to land, and he was off by only 5%, you would land in a different country—or at least several states away from where you wanted to go! Even only 5% off is significant and has a profound effect in your life—for good or for bad. What is your 5% doing for you? How is it sabotaging other areas in your life?

This is not about upsetting people. It is about raising your awareness. What can you find that is 5% out of alignment in your integrity? I promise I have not found even one person who could not find something. Raise your integrity, and change your life instantly! How might you up-level your integrity?

I put all integrity into two categories—Inconsistent Integrity and Impeccable Integrity.

Inconsistent Integrity is just that—inconsistent. It is having integrity most of the time, but includes times that you say you will do something and then don't, or you borrow something without returning it. You say you will pay someone and then you don't, or you pay it late. It is paying your bills late, or showing up late and unprepared for a meeting or engagement. It is not waiting your turn in line and finding ways to get ahead of others. It is taking things that do not belong to you—office supplies, or other items from work that you did not pay for. It is spending time on social media when you are at work or on the time clock, or answering personal emails while being paid to do a job for someone else. It is saying you will call someone and not doing it. It is using bad language in one group of people and pretending to be something else for a different group of people. It is lowering your standards or not living up to the standards you have set for yourself. It is doing things that you are not proud of, or are even ashamed of, in secret. It is not honoring yourself and not being all that you could be. This list could go on forever.

Impeccable Integrity, on the other hand, is much different. Impeccable means to be in accordance with the highest standards, faultless, flawless, irreproachable, perfect, and exemplary. Sounds pretty much impossible, right? No. We can always be striving for Impeccable Integrity. It does require work, focus, and commitment. Many aspects come to mind:

- Keep Your Word
- Live in Honor
- Be Punctual
- Keep all Commitments
- Be Honest, Always
- Live in Happiness
- Be Respectful
- Follow Through
- Be Worthy
- Love Unconditionally
- Be Prepared
- Be Giving and Kind
- Be True to You
- Honor Your Values
- Obey the Law
- Live the Code of Ethics

To have perfect integrity is impossible. Nobody's perfect. But to be continuously perfecting our Integrity is powerful. That means we are constantly tweaking and improving ourselves, and being conscious of where we can change our focus to create a different outcome.

The acronym I use for Integrity is IMPLEMENT.

Implement Impeccable Integrity

I=Influence: You are always being watched, therefore you are always of influence. Good or bad—you are influential. Higher levels of influence have higher levels of integrity. Our influence is important and should be held in the highest esteem possible.

M=Measure: Know your values. Align your beliefs. Consistently measure your results. Consistently measure your results with what is working and not working. When we measure, we are taking an accounting, and using our results to tell us what is going on—what is working and what is not working.

P=Perfect: Nobody's perfect, but Perfecting where you are, and moving toward taking it to the next level is valuable. When we are perfecting our self and raising our self to a higher level, we are becoming as close to perfect as we can.

L=Lead: Become the leader you would follow! Lead by example. Live the qualities you would want to see in your leader. Hold yourself to that same standard of leadership. You do not have to be the manager to be a leader in the group. You do not need to be in the front of a line to lead the group. Lead from where you are.

E=Examine: Be willing to take a look inside and examine where you are and where you would like to be. Assess and do what is right. Not what is easy! Keep your word. Examine where you are out of alignment, and make a plan on what you get to do to change it.

M=Mindset: You get to have your mindset right and on board with you. You get to decide what it looks like, and what you want to do about it. You are choosing every choice that is made for you, so make your choices count. Stop justification and the blame game. Be accountable and responsible.

E=Empower: Empower yourself with an inner sense of wholeness. People are watching—be an inspiration to empower them to a higher level of integrity too. Align your integrity and see the results in your life. Share your experience with others to empower them to take action in their life.

N=Nurture: Nurture and be good to yourself. Be forgiving. This is a process, not perfection. Nurture yourself through the process. It will not always be easy, but it will always be worth it. Trust this process and celebrate your success often.

T=Transform: Be true to you! You will reach new levels and see transformation in your life. Raise the bar and watch yourself transform in all areas. This truly will lead to transformation in many areas in your life, and will align you on your path of personal growth and potential.

When I talk with people about this particular trait, I get a lot of pushback. I just ask you to look at it for what it is worth. This is not Kris in judgment telling you how to live your life, but rather having a frank conversation with you to help you perhaps raise the bar and up-level your integrity. Raising your awareness will enhance your life.

Story: Chamber Lady

I was speaking for a Women in Business Multi-Chamber Event. I love to have audience interaction, and was having an activity that had this audience participating with me. I was speaking on integrity. We were having a very frank conversation and I began pushing buttons with the group. A woman in the group felt I had really pushed her buttons, and she began giving me some pushback on it. Some of you might want to call that an argument or anger—I call it pushback. When you feel upset, resistance, or pushback on something, you should always examine it, because it is giving you feedback. Feedback is how we are able to see what could be us out of alignment.

How many times in our lives have we heard the term “tough love” or “the truth hurts”? This is a time to examine things further. Find out why it is a sensitive issue for you, without being in judgement or placing blame on the person that brought it to your attention. Recognize it, evaluate it, and then decide your next step. If we are willing to not be easily offended, allowing ourselves to consider the feedback without emotion, and really take a deep look—it can be the most powerful thing for us. Yes, there are a ton of people out there who are just coming from their ego and giving us bad feedback. That is when it is about them, rather than real feedback for us.

The lady from the Chamber event spoke her peace. She brought her rationalization into why she drives over the speed limit, and even gave me pushback on the cell phone issues we had brought up too. When the event was over, she came over and talked with me personally. She definitely had her buttons pushed, but in a way that I felt would allow her to take a closer examination of her life.

Two weeks later, I received a thank-you card in the mail. I opened it and read it. It was from my Chamber lady. She said she actually put into action what I had talked about. She took a good look at her life, and evaluated where she had been justifying things. She decided to start with some things I had talked about in raising her personal integrity. She said her entire world changed! She thanked me for pushing her buttons and assisting her to take a deeper look into herself and her own levels of integrity. Crazy, right? Wrong. I have clients and attendees who have heard me speak or have been at an event, people who have watched videos on my YouTube channel, or even those who have read my book, that send me messages of thanks for bringing this to their attention. Thanking me for pushing their buttons.

How might you up-level your integrity?

"Integrity is doing what is right always—not what is simply easier." ~Kris Barney

Chapter 20

What Are Ethics Anyway

"The time is always right to do what is right." ~Martin Luther King

Let's start off by defining work ethic. There are all kinds of definitions attached to this phrase, and many different interpretations. The simple definition of work ethic is "a set of moral principles that an employee uses in the performance of their job." Yet, another definition describes work ethic as "the belief in the moral benefit and importance of work and its inherent ability to strengthen character."

Work ethic can refer to how you feel about your job—it includes your attitude and behavior. It is also about how you do your job, and the responsibilities that come with your position or title. Ethics is how you communicate and interact with others, as well as the level of respect you show others at work. Ethics is having key characteristics within you—such as humility, empathy, honesty, accountability, and integrity. It really is true that how you act on the job will reveal your work ethics. Your strength of character is easily shown when the going gets tough. And if you are not living in this way, it will show up!

It is one thing to declare you have a strong work ethic. But it is another totally different thing to convince those around you that you really do have a strong work ethic.

In fact, most leaders are not inclined to take your claims at face value. Instead, they prefer that you convince them with actions and not just words.

For all intents and purposes, we could say this: **Ethics = Values + Choices + Actions**

Highest Standards & Honorable Character are your best Assets. Yet isn't that just good Ethics? ~Kris Barney

It is crucial to have a strong work ethic if you desire to have or hold a leadership position. It requires you to be a positive person and to look for the good in others. As you develop exceptional ethics, you naturally are influential and will almost automatically be advanced in your career. Don't all big business people want all of the qualities in an employee that we mentioned above? YES!

Business owners want leaders they can trust, those who can be put in charge of teams or huge projects. They do not want to babysit or have to deal with issues. They want leaders with strong traits, strong character, and people with vision to see the possibilities. They want someone who is task and goal oriented, and can lead by example. They do not want to be told from you that you are ethical. They want to see this in action in all that you do. When they recognize these qualities in you, that is when you get promoted and advanced in your career. To dramatically progress up the ranks of the organization, raise your level of work ethics.

Story: The Overachiever

I have a son who did not really fit the 'high school teenager' mold. He was very driven and focused, and liked things at his own pace. He did not have time for projects, or even classes for that matter, to waste his time. I learned early on in his life that when he said, "I was thinking..." it was usually followed by how his way to do the particular chore or project we were doing, would work more efficient and would be faster or a better plan. He was usually right.

Beings he was the 'little brother'—he was the third boy born in three and a half years—the older, wiser brothers did not always appreciate his input. These three boys were incredible! Yes, I am biased! When they were in high school, my husband and I helped set them up in business. They named their business after what everyone was calling them. They were the *Hard Workin' Fools*!

All three boys worked incredibly hard in this company. They even ran crews of their own, doing tear-down work on fix-and-flip housing projects, laying sod, doing skid steer work, and anything in between. It was a happy day when the third son turned 16 and got his driver's license, because then he could run his own crew and not have to have anyone else in charge of him. He was very driven and quite confident. Of course, I did raise them all to be this way. Their business was extremely successful. It made them lots of money and employed several other high school boys that proved they could keep up with the company name of *Hard Workin' Fools*! To this day, all three sons are very successful, very driven, and are fantastic providers for their families. They make this momma very proud.

My youngest son decided that regular high school was not for him, and chose to go to an accelerated early college high school. Two years later, he graduated with his Associates Degree as a senior in high school. He was also awarded a huge scholarship to a very prestigious local college. Three years later, he not only had earned his Bachelor's degree, but he had earned his Master's Degree in Accounting before his 21st birthday. Can you say overachiever?

But it is what he did from there that I want to draw your attention to. At 21 years old, he was paid well to transfer out of state to open up a training department in the company that he worked for. He did this. He showed unbelievable work ethic, and worked extremely hard to prove himself, as he was the young kid training people old enough to be his parents. His superiors even suggested he wear glasses instead of contacts, because it made him look older.

He worked diligently and held the highest standards possible when it came to ethics. He held himself to incredible standards and created great things in every department where he was part of the team. Recently, at 29 years old, he has been put in charge of teams and even huge budgets with tons of responsibility. Yes he is smart. Yes he is driven. But above all, he holds his work ethic and standards at the highest level possible, and he is seen as a leader. He influences many. He is seen for his value because he puts ethics first—always.

I tell you this not to brag—although, as a mother I love to brag about all of my fantastic kiddos and grandkiddos! But I tell you this because, as a business owner for 35 years myself, I have watched him climb this ladder quickly. I have experienced his level of ownership in always holding his standards to the highest level, and keeping his work ethic as a major focus. Ethics and values have been held to the highest standard with him, and it has paid off big time!

When he reads this part in my book, he will not be happy that I told his story. Yet, I am inspired as I have watched him achieve the high level of stewardship and management in his career, and I hope that it inspires you too. I joke and tease him, calling him my little overachiever, because he will always be my baby boy.

What is possible for you? How could you raise your work ethics, and what would you gain by doing it?

We have talked a lot about ethics and we have also talked a lot about integrity in this section. I believe Chris Karcher said it best:

"Integrity is choosing your thoughts and actions based on values and beliefs, rather than personal gain."

When we are doing it because it is the right thing to do, we are rewarded. When we are doing things for the wrong reason, it shows up.

Here is a list that we can pay attention to when it comes to being ethical:

- Having a high level of integrity
- Being honest in all dealings
- Living high standards
- Doing quality work
- Being punctual and respectful
- Working well with others
- Being responsible and accountable
- Being dedicated to the company
- Being respectful of others
- Building trust with others
- Developing strong relationships
- Being self-disciplined and taking action
- Being energetic and positive
- Being knowledgeable and willing to learn
- Creating positive results

- Willing to do what it takes
- Hitting deadlines ahead of schedule
- Working well with others and being a team player
- Avoiding gossip and office drama, being fair with others
- Going the extra mile
- Being organized and structured
- Being health conscious, with strong body and mind
- Being a good listener, and valuing others' opinions
- Doing quality work and not wasting time
- Putting the company first
- Following the rules and company standards
- Being consistent and performing well
- Having great time management skills
- Outperforming the competition
- Having high standard of professionalism
- Completing duties and responsibilities
- Seeing the good in others, wanting others to succeed

This is a long list. It is probably not the most comprehensive list, but rather a great place to start. This list can be a bit overwhelming, but in reality these things listed are not that difficult to do. You are probably already doing most of them, and if you are not, this is great feedback as to where you can start to focus and improve.

When we are exceptional in our character, it creates noteworthy performance and the highest professionalism—which in turn, is simply good ethics. Isn't that what we are striving for?

How would living in this way in your personal life change your relationships and even your family life? Ethics is not just a part-time job that we live only for others to see—it is who we are, and what we stand for always, in everything. Ethics are your moral principles and character, and they show up naturally. They are who we really are.

"Influence comes through your example of being ethical and full of integrity in all that you do." ~Kris Barney

Chapter 21

A Year to Remember

"Your Life is Your Message to the World. Make Sure it's Inspiring!" ~ Anonymous

Many years after the suicide death of my twin brother, his youngest son had reached a point that he could not be handled by his mother or his grandparents—which had been the ones that had been caring for him for the last few years. I received a phone call from my mother. She said, "He is just too big and too strong, and we are too old to be able to handle him."

At this point in his life, he was over six feet tall and well over 200 pounds. He was strong as an ox, and there were times that he honestly kind of acted like one. That was the phone call that brought me to the point of feeling that it was time for our family to step up to the plate, and take my nephew into our home.

Seriously, I think we may have had brain damage. This was a 15-year-old troubled teenager. He had a police record, and had just been kicked out of his high school. This was not the first school to do that. He was at the end of his sophomore year, and only had .5 of a credit as far as passing his classes for almost two years. Graduating looked impossible.

To be fair, this kid had not had a fighting chance. He

struggled with Asperger's, which had gone misdiagnosed. His father had killed himself when he was three-and-a-half years old. His mother had remarried, but several years later, he and his step-dad could not be under the same roof. At this point, for the better part of four years, he had been passed around and had not really belonged anywhere. As a family, we decided to take him in. We became certified to do foster care for him, and began our journey together in 2011. After all, this poor kid deserved to be loved and cared about and have someone in his corner!

This same year was our daughter's senior year in high school. She was enrolled in a charter school and they accepted my nephew into their school as well. She was pretty much in the opposite direction from her cousin. She was holding a large leadership position at school. She was in the school play, an editor of the yearbook, a leader in most of her classes, and getting good grades as an honor student. She was extremely busy! We also had our middle son find his sweetheart, and we had a wedding in August 2011. Typical family stuff, I know. But when you put it all together, it feels a bit overwhelming.

Taking in my nephew came with many challenges. It pushed our buttons in areas that we never even imagined. But it was good. He was doing very well in school, and over time, he graduated on time and even earned his Eagle Scout award. We came to love him as our own, and were exceptionally proud of him and his accomplishments—even when the struggles and challenges brought tears and frustration.

My oldest son had just purchased a home in July 2011. It was a bank-owned property that he got a great deal on it. He had a lot of work to do to get it like he wanted. He spent many hours stripping out carpeting, pulling down the drywall, and taking the basement clear down to the studs. Being single and 25 years old, he had time on his hands, and was a strong strapping man—excited to be working on his own home.

Our family loves to play together! We have had a motto for years, it goes like this: "Families that play together, stay together!" We also have a motto of, "When we work, we work hard. And when we play, we play hard too!" It was no different than usual to find ourselves at the Sand Dunes for a holiday weekend for Labor Day, September 2011.

My oldest son had decided he was a "big boy" now, and no longer had to have mother's permission to ride a motorcycle versus a hopped-up four wheeler. Crazy how kids think that, right? This trip to the dunes was the maiden voyage on his new motorcycle. Long story short, while climbing Sand Mountain at the Jericho Sand Dunes, he had an accident and broke his back.

Recovery of his broken back took many weeks. He had complications, and a lot of severe headaches. But he was able to return to work eight weeks later, the beginning of November, on 'light duty.'

We are the family that loves to play, so that year for Thanksgiving, we decided to take out all of the Rock Crawlers and go camping and Rock Crawling in Moab, Utah. As we made the five hour drive to get there, my oldest son's headaches were so severe that he had to have his younger brother drive his rig for him—as he could hardly sit up straight. As the days progressed, his headaches did not get better, and he was almost unable to even go on rides with us. He could not even be upright because the pain and nausea were so bad, and he had now lost the site out of his right eye.

We returned from our trip and went straight to the brain surgeon that had been following us for many years now. He was immediately scheduled for an MRI of his brain. The test results were in. He had a brain tumor! It was so severe that they scheduled him for brain tumor removal surgery immediately. That was the first week of December.

Surgery went well. They told us they got it all and that it was benign. We were thrilled! It was the best case scenario at this point. His sight in his eye returned, and his recovery went very smooth. Eight weeks later, he returned again to work at his job on light duty.

He worked three days. On the morning of the fourth day, he collapsed at work! His boss drove him home and met me there, and I took him back into the brain surgeon's office. He immediately sent us for another MRI of his brain. THE BRAIN TUMOR WAS BACK! It had only been eight and a half weeks!!

He underwent the second brain tumor removal surgery on Feb 8th, 2012. This time it did not go so well. He came out of surgery completely deaf. He could not hear anything. This was caused by the swelling in his brain. The doctor had determined that the tumor had grown back in that short eight weeks. This brain tumor was after him with a vengeance!

At this point, he was well past having any work benefits. We had to put him on extremely expensive COBRA health insurance, while we were paying thousands in medical bills and trying to keep his house. The stressors were pretty high at this point, as you can well imagine. We went through another eight weeks of recovery. He then had to pass testing to keep his job, as he still had no hearing. He was pretty frail because he had a broken back and two brain surgeries in less than six months. And he was struggling personally, as he had no income. We had to sell all kinds of toys, like his motorcycle, four-wheeler, rock crawler, trailer, and even his fifth wheel trailer—just to keep him a float and keep his home. As his parents, we also had been on a selling frenzy, downsizing and getting things sold to help with expenses, and simplifying since we were about to become empty nesters.

Things were pretty tough. I was working really hard to care for my nephew, get my daughter graduated from high school, keep my oldest child alive, enjoy the newlyweds, be self-employed, and keep the business running. You can imagine how much sleep I was getting, and the level of stress that was going on around our house.

I got a phone call one day from my oldest son. This was rare, as he could not hear a thing at this point, so it was useless to have a phone call—we had gotten good at texting. I answered the phone. He said, "I can hear!" He had been driving his work truck around, and all of the sudden, he could hear the stereo playing! Miraculously, he had about 40% of his hearing return. We were thrilled! He was ecstatic!

A couple weeks later, in April, he called me and said, "Mom, I am losing my sight in my right eye again." How could this be happening? My heart ached for my poor son!

We again went in for an MRI. I want you to imagine yourself sitting in the brain surgeon's office with your child ... The doctor enters the room. He walks over and leans back onto the counter then crosses his legs. That is when I notice the tear in his eye. He then says, "The Brain Tumor is back." For a third time in just five months! This brain tumor was never benign. It was full blown cancerous. We had the third surgery in June 2012. It was followed by gamma knife radiation. It was a horrific few months. The tumor had invaded the optic nerve at this point, and the only way to save his sight in the left eye, was to radiate, and that would permanently take away the sight in his right eye. The doctor's best guess for how long he could go without the surgery was a best case scenario of about two months to live. We chose to do the third brain surgery, and to permanently lose his eyesight in one eye, rather than for him to be blind in both. It was an unbelievable choice. Honestly it sucked!

During this entire year, we had a lot of support from family and friends. We had incredible support from his work and our neighbors. We had quite a bit of this experience out there on Facebook and social media. The night before the third brain tumor surgery, I learned a big lesson. I went on Facebook. I began by thanking those praying for us and for all of their support, but pretty much, I was complaining that my son had to go through this again. I talked about the stress, all he had been through, and pretty much posted a victim post out there to all my friends and followers.

As I scrolled down several posts after posting my own post—my son had also posted just a few minutes before me. He wrote, "I am in Gratitude for the opportunity that I have to get to know my Savior better through all of these trials & difficulties! I am humbled and grateful to all of you that have prayed and cared so much for me."

What an incredible example he was to ME! He truly is my HERO! This lesson came with a slap in the face. I knew better than this. After all, I had taught him those qualities and traits. I got to take a good look at this. There was definitely some feedback for me to look at. I was so proud of him and the example he was being for literally thousands of people.

We rounded the corner in August. My oldest son moved back into his home and could now care for himself pretty well. We had gotten his house finished, and the newlyweds moved into his basement apartment to help him out. My youngest son had transferred to Arizona for work, and was now a homeowner there. My daughter moved out and away to college, about three and a half hours away from home. My nephew reached a point that he got to move in with another family. In the matter of less than a week, I went from being needed—to keep one son alive, to counsel one daughter for big life decisions, to care for a nephew 24/7 (who was now living somewhere else, and I would only have him overnight on Wednesdays and every other weekend)—to not being needed at all. My husband was very self-sufficient and had become pretty good at our situation due to our circumstances over the last year. I was seriously not needed at all! That was tough to take.

I wallowed in my pity party for a few weeks. I felt sad and discouraged. I was lonely. I loved being a mom—and after the past year, I did not know what I would do. Yes, we still had our business, but we had gone through a rough deal with business investing, and had lost a ton of money the year prior to this. I knew that at some point, I would get to decide what my next thing would be.

Three weeks later, on the way to spend a week at Lake Powell on our houseboat, I received a phone call. It was someone telling me I had won tickets to her three day event. The catch was that it would be in Scottsdale, Arizona. The dates were September 27th-30th, 2012. That was about ten days away. I spent an amazing week at Lake Powell and then called her to say that I would be attending. After all, my son who lived in the Phoenix area had his birthday on September 26th! I could fly in a day early, and spend his birthday with him. I could stay with him at his house and I could use his car. It was a great plan.

I attended this conference. My life as I knew it was never the same. It was a great conference, but it was not the conference that changed me. We were just a few hours into the conference when I knew that I was to be a public speaker. This was not EVER on my radar before this in my life! I had talked with a few attendees about our last year, and the trials we had been through, and I was asked, “Why are you not sharing your story?” During our first lunch hour, I called my husband and told him that I was now going to be a professional speaker! The rest is HISTORY.

The **7 Traits** that I teach, and have written about in this book, are what I had to do to get through all of the tough things we have faced. It is what I had to do to be self-employed for 35 years. It is what I have had to embrace when I needed to up-level and create the change needed in my life. It is what I have had to embody to create change.

Taking inspired action is a requirement. Doing nothing is not acceptable. You have the ability to do anything you put your mind to. Today is a great day to make the changes you want in your life. May you know that you are on the right path. You can do this. We all have our challenges and trials that push our buttons, yet we all have the opportunity to choose how we want to handle it. May you find joy in your journey as you embrace the **7 Traits**, and may you have all the success you have ever dreamed of.

You are incredible! You are worth it! You are enough!

"Exceptional character creates noteworthy performance and the highest professionalism." ~Kris Barney

CONCLUSION

Thank you for being here with me. I have loved having you here. I have given you much to think about, and a whole world of ideas and direction—if you are committed to create change in your life. I know this works. I am living proof of it. I have not only lived it, I have taught it to literally thousands of people and been blessed to see the difference it has made in their lives. This is a continuous work. We can continually grow and improve if we have the desire to be more, to have more, and are willing to take that deep look within and recognize where we deserve to make change happen.

Let's recap the **7 Traits** to Change Your Life and Your World:

- SHOW Sincere Service
- GROW in Genuine Gratitude
- CREATE Courageous Confidence
- EXCEL in Exceptional Excellence
- LIVE in Lasting Love
- CONNECT with Complete Communication
- IMPLEMENT Impeccable Integrity

I know that when you incorporate these seven traits into your life, you will see a profound impact in your own life and the lives around you. You will see improvement beyond measure. It is because you will be blessing the lives of others by serving and loving them, that your life will be blessed in return. As you up-level your own life, you will get out of your own way. Your focus will shift and become very clear on just how you can go to the next level. You will find your thoughts lingering in an outward focus, and will be inspired to reach out to certain people. You will also be inspired as to what may be your next step in this process. Be open and trusting of yourself in this process. Be true to your beliefs and your character. Own your self-worth and know that you are enough! May you implement these simple traits into your life, and may you find true happiness, peace, freedom, and abundance! Life is amazing as we follow these universal truths and see that "All Things Are Possible."

I have literally watched leaders improve. I have seen people as they become more influential. I have witnessed countless opportunities come to them, as they change and improve, and commit to stepping up to a new level of integrity and excellence. This has shown up in advancements at work, up-leveling in their business, doubling and even tripling revenue. As your team becomes more effective, they become more productive. When productivity improves, profits raise. It is through these universal truths and traits that this happens. As we raise the bar, community is formed in the workplace, respect is raised, and we feel a sense of belonging in a new and heightened way. Relationships are improved and enhanced as we embrace these traits and raise our excellence and confidence. Trust is formed with not only ourselves, but with all our significant relationships and with our co-workers, our colleges, our managers, and our teams.

Where do you start making some changes? First, list three action items in each of the traits. They do not need to be huge items, but all of us have areas in which we need to do some general house cleaning—making simple but profound changes. What are the first three things that come to mind? Write them down and make a plan to implement those changes this week. The sooner you begin, the sooner you see CHANGE!

I would love to receive feedback from you. I love hearing how others are creating better lives through making conscious decisions and being conscious of their choices. E-mail and tell me how this is working for you at connections@allthingspossible.biz.

I would like to invite you to join me on YouTube. Go to Kris Barney. We just uploaded episode #208 in our videos! Our videos are on a variety of topics—from Time Management, my 7 Traits, Leadership, Communication, Personal Development, Self-improvement, Confidence, Excellence, Integrity, Relationships, to Health and Healing. Please subscribe to our channel so you will be notified when we post a new episode.

To see more about me and my speaking and training, go to my website www.krisbarney.com. You can easily see if I am a good fit for your organization as a Keynote speaker or trainer. I would also love it if you could share this with someone you feel would benefit from this book, or an organization that would benefit from bringing me into their organization.

My company is: All Things Possible, Inc. You can join our community there at www.allthingspossible.biz. On this website, you can opt in to get your free gift. This will also get you access to my weekly newsletter with tips and stories on how life can be better, and how you can be more empowered, engaged, and influential. What you will find, if you haven't already learned this from reading my book, is that I am very open and authentic in sharing with you real life stories of successes and failures, and those valuable lessons learned.

I want to leave you with this:

"Your decisions today have the power to determine the outcome of the rest of your life. Will today be the day that your decisions become your defining moment? ~Kris Barney

With Light, Love, and Abundance to you all! It's goodbye for now from me, Kris Barney.

Quotes

Chapter 1

"The best way to find yourself is to lose yourself in the service of others." ~Mahatma Gandhi

"Only a life lived in the service of others is worth living." ~ Albert Einstein

"It's the little things we do, on a consistent basis, that ultimately change our lives!" ~Kris Barney

Chapter 2

"Your greatest test is when you are able to bless someone else, while you are going through your own storm." ~Zig Ziglar

"Everyone has the power within them to conquer any challenge life throws at them, and be stronger because of it!" ~Kris Barney

Chapter 3

"You never know how strong you are, until being strong is your only choice. Cowboy Up!" ~Jesse Barney

"Challenges will come to all of us. How we choose to see and handle them will determine if we go through them and learn, or simply endure them." ~Kris Barney

Chapter 4

"Gratitude and complaining cannot co-exist simultaneously; you must choose the ONE that best serves you!" ~Hal Elrod

"Gratitude is the single most important ingredient to living a successful and fulfilling life." ~Jack Canfield

"Gratitude is the Ultimate Magnifier. To Change Your Life Immediately, Focus on Being Grateful." ~Kris Barney

Chapter 5

"As we express our gratitude, we must never forget that the highest appreciation is not to utter words, but to live them." ~John F. Kennedy

"When you are Grateful, fear disappears and abundance appears." ~Tony Robbins

"Fear can stop you or propel you—the choice is yours." ~Kris Barney

"Freedom is the opportunity to Be More than you were before, to Have More, and to Become More. It is the Absence of Fear…True Freedom comes from Within." ~Kris Barney

Chapter 6

"Gratitude is the single most important ingredient to living a successful and fulfilling life." ~Jack Canfield

"I don't have to chase extraordinary moments to find happiness—it's right in front of me if I'm paying attention and practicing gratitude." ~Brene Brown

"The Universe provides abundantly when you're in a state of Gratefulness." ~Wayne Dyer

"Empathy and Gratitude allow us to go Beyond just Being Compassionate and Thankful. They allow us to build Trust, Honor, and Respect." ~Kris Barney

Chapter 7

"Vulnerability is our most accurate measurement of courage." ~Brene Brown

"Courageous Confidence is something you create within yourself by believing in who you are and who you are meant to be!" ~Kris Barney

Chapter 8

"You must learn a new way to think before you can master a new way to be." ~Marianne Williamson

"Change Your Inner Dialog and Watch how Fast Your

Confidence Grows." ~Kris Barney

"We Create Our Own Reality when we Recognize what we are Doing and make the Corrections needed—we are Happier, Healthier, and more Confident." ~Kris Barney

Chapter 9

"When one door of happiness closes, another opens; but often we look so long at the closed door that we do not see the one which has been opened for us." Helen Keller

"Happiness comes from valuing, appreciating, and acknowledging what we have—rather than focusing on what is missing." ~Kris Barney

Chapter 10

"We are what we repeatedly do; therefore Excellence is not an act but a habit." Aristotle

"You must learn a new way to think before you can master a new way to be." ~Marianne Williamson

"Change Your Inner Dialog and Watch how Fast Your Confidence Grows." ~Kris Barney

Chapter 11

"Treat a man as he is and he will remain as he is. Treat a man as he can and should be, and he will become as he can and should be." ~Stephen R. Covey

"My mother said to me, 'If you become a soldier, you'll be a general. If you become a monk, you'll end up as the pope.' Instead, I became a painter, and wound up as Picasso." ~Pablo Picasso

"Exceptional Excellence is living your full potential, while inspiring others to do the same." ~Kris Barney

Chapter 12

"No matter how many mistakes you make, or how slow you proGress, you're still way ahead of everyone who isn't trying." ~Tony Robbins

"Everyone has the power within them to conquer any challenge life throws at them and be stronger because of it!" ~Kris Barney

Chapter 13

"Needless to say, you can love people without leading them, but you cannot lead people without loving them." I do know this to be true! ~John Maxwell

"We all know that LOVE is the greatest power in the Universe. Why do we not take advantage of it in all areas of our life? It can be so simple, and yet we make it difficult." ~Kris Barney

Chapter 14

"We are not held back by the love we didn't receive in the past, but by the love we're not extending in the present." ~Marianne Williamson

"It takes a lot more courage to let something go than it does to hang onto it, trying to make it better. Letting go doesn't mean ignoring a situation. Letting go means accepting what is, exactly as it is, without fear, resistance, or a struggle for control." ~Tyanla Vanzant

"Stop hating yourself because of what you are not yet. Start loving yourself for what you are right now." ~Kris Barney

Chapter 15

"Let today be the day you love yourself enough to no longer just dream of a better life; let today be the day you act upon it." ~Steve Maraboli

"You yourself, as much as anybody in the entire universe, deserve your love and affection." ~Budda

"Your Decisions Today Have the Power to Determine the Outcome of the Rest of Your Life. Will Today Be the Day That Your Decision Becomes Your Defining Moment?" ~Kris Barney

Chapter 16

"Communication is a skill that you can learn. It's like riding a bicycle or typing. If you're willing to work at it, you can rapidly improve the quality of every part of your life." ~Brian Tracy.

"Communication —the human connection—is the key to personal and career success." ~Paul Meyer

"Communication is like a backbone. It is required if we want to be successful!" ~Kris Barney

Chapter 17

"Your ability to communicate is an important tool in your pursuit of your goals, whether it is with your family, your co-workers, or your clients and customers." ~Les Brown

"Trust is the glue of life. It's the most essential ingredient in effective communication. It's the foundational principle that holds all relationships." ~Stephen Covey

"If you just communicate, you can get by. But if you communicate skillfully, you can work miracles." ~Jim Rohn

"Good Communication is so much more than just words—it is our actions and our ability to listen. It is communicating clearly and being understood." ~Kris Barney

Chapter 18

"The biggest communication problem is we do not listen to understand. We listen to reply." ~Zig Ziglar

"The quality of your Communication is the quality of your life." ~Tony Robbins

"Effective Communication begins and ends with intentional listening!" ~Kris Barney

Chapter 19

"Real Integrity is doing the right thing, knowing that nobody's going to know whether you did it or not." ~Oprah Winfrey

"Integrity is doing what is right always—not what is simply easier." ~Kris Barney

"I have found that we create our reality. And when we recognize what we are doing, and make the corrections needed—we can be happier, healthier, and more successful!" ~Kris Barney

Chapter 20

"The time is always right to do what is right." ~Martin Luther King

"Integrity is choosing your thoughts and actions based on values and beliefs, rather than personal gain." ~Chris Karcher

"Highest Standards & Honorable Character are your best Assets. Yet isn't that just good Ethics?" ~Kris Barney

"Influence comes through your example of being ethical and full of integrity in all that you do." ~Kris Barney

Chapter 21

"Your Life is Your Message to the World. Make Sure it's Inspiring!" ~Anonymous

"Exceptional character creates noteworthy performance and the highest professionalism." ~Kris Barney

Testimonials

“Kris Barney is a **phenomenal speaker**, insightful thinker, and an even better person. She has the ability to make you **think introspectively**, understand the need for improvement, and provide the tools to make it happen. Kris has lived her content and because of that, **she speaks it from the heart.**”

~Ty Bennett- CSP Speaker, Author, & Entrepreneur, Leadership Inc.

“Kris was a dynamic speaker who shared empowering insights while having the frank discussion that allows you to implement the changes needed to experience lasting success.”

~Dr. Tom Grant, Jr., DC

"Kris Barney is a ***Dynamic, Authentic Speaker*** who shares her own unique content that comes from her heart and experience! Definitely check her out! Even a month after she was our ***Keynote Speaker,*** the ladies in our group were still talking about Kris and what they learned from her!"

~Mandy Pratt, Director of eWomen Network, Boise ID

“Kris Barney was a fantastic **Keynote Speaker** for a Grief Group at **Intermountain Medical Center**. She shared from her heart, her experiences and practical insights to move the audience forward in their lives. She connected with us on a very deep level and delivered phenomenal content. We went from laughter to tears as we moved through a fantastic experience."

~Tiffany Berg Coughran, Certified Chaplain, Professional Consultant SLC, UT

"Kris Barney is an inspiring and thought provoking speaker. She opens your mind to the idea of personal integrity and how it plays out in everything we do in life. What an incredibly frank but powerful message that will up-level every person in our audience! Thank you Kris for opening the conversation and providing some wonderful nuggets to live by!"

~Jevine Lane, President and CEO West Jordan Chamber of Commerce

Kris has excellent content, and delivers it with energy and enthusiasm. The audience was engaged, and loved her! I highly recommend Kris for your event.

~Lori Barland **eWomenNetwork, Salt Lake Managing Director**

Kris is a **POWERHOUSE** with a big heart! I learned so much from her, not just listening to her courage as she walks through huge challenges, but how it has changed me. She has taught me so much and dissolved my excuses, all while giving me the tools that I can implement immediately. Thank you Kris for being a BOLD, REFRESHING voice of truth for REAL CHANGE!

~Marla Dee, Creator of Clear & Simple Organizing

About the Author

Kris Barney is a successful entrepreneur, multi-faceted trainer, and a leadership and communication expert. She has coached hundreds of individuals that range from entrepreneurs to corporate executives. Her speaking has put her in front of a diverse range of clients. Her keynotes *Leadership from the Inside Out, Delete the Divide,* and *Stuck Sucks—Discover the Gifts in Your Garbage,* have been well received by corporate leaders, entrepreneurs, and small business owners, alike.

Her online TV channel, All Things Possible TV, has been downloaded over 250,000 times, and has allowed Kris to share her expertise with hundreds of thousands of people around the world. She is passionate about training. She has put in over 6500 hours in training and certifications. Her work's focus lies in leadership and communication, as she believes they are the cornerstones to effective organizations.

She has successfully built and run four companies in four distinct industries. The breadth of her experience gives her a unique vantage point that allows her to customize her message and relate to leaders' struggles, while leading them to solutions.

Kris Barney has the knowledge, experience and expertise to strengthen and empower others to trust, love, and believe in themselves. She specializes in conquering the tough challenges while strengthening and healing relationships—and creating balance and confidence to live a joyful, rewarding, and purpose-filled life of Love, Joy, and Peace.

Kris has been married to the love of her life, Bill Barney, for 35 years. She is the mother of four amazing children, four dynamic in-laws, and four exceptional grandchildren. She loves making memories to last a lifetime!